THE PUFFIN CANADIAN BEGINNER'S DICTIONARY

Compiled by Rosemary Sansome

Illustrated by Susan Shields and Hope Mount

CANADIAN EDITOR

K. J. WEBER

Diane Hanano

Puffin Books

by arrangement with Oxford University Press

Puffin Books
The Puffin Canadian Beginner's Dictionary

This dictionary is intended primarily for six to nine year-olds. It contains approximately 4,800 headwords and over 300 additional items in supplementary lists. All the headwords are defined simply and clearly in terms of a vocabulary of less than 2,000 words. Each sense of a word is numbered separately and begins on a fresh line.

The words chosen for inclusion are those most likely to be needed by children in this age-range. Accordingly, irregular or difficult plural and verbal forms have been included only in terms of their likely usage at this level.

Examples of usage are provided wherever appropriate and are printed in italics.

Simple pronunciation guides are given for words with difficult or ambiguous pronunciations.

The names of days, months, numbers, shapes, colours, planets, continents, peoples and places are listed separately at the end of the book. Some are also included in the body of the dictionary.

K.J. Weber has taught for more than twenty years and is the former chairman of the Department of Special Education at the University of Toronto. He has been in demand as a speaker not only in Canada, but also in Europe and at the United Nations. His books are used in over fifty countries.

Penguin Books Canada Ltd., 2801 John Street, Markham, Ontario, Canada L3R 1B4
Penguin Books Ltd., 27 Wrights Lane, London W8 5TZ (Publishing & Editorial)
and Harmondsworth, Middlesex, England (Distribution & Warehouse)
Penguin Books, 40 West 23rd Street, New York 10010, U.S.A.
Penguin Books Australia Ltd., Ringwood, Victoria, Australia
Penguin Books (N.Z.) Ltd., 182–190 Wairau Road, Auckland 10, New Zealand

First published by Oxford University Press 1978
Published in Puffin Books 1982
Canadian edition published in Puffin Books 1984
Reprinted 1986, 1987 (twice)

Copyright © Oxford University Press, 1978
Illustrations copyright © Susan Shields, 1982 and Hope Mount, 1984.
All rights reserved.

Manufactured in Canada by Friesen Printers
Typesetting by Art-U Graphics

Canadian Cataloguing in Publication Data
Weber, K. J. (Kenneth Jerome), 1940-
   Puffin Canadian beginner's dictionary

ISBN 0-14-031698-1

1. English language — Dictionaries, Juvenile. I. Title.

PE3235.W42   j423   C83-098755-X

Aa

aardvark an animal with large ears and a long nose. It is sometimes called an anteater.

abandon to leave forever

abbey 1 a big, old church
2 a place where monks or nuns live or work

abbreviation a short way of writing a word or a group of words
*NHL is an **abbreviation** for National Hockey League.*

ability the power to do something

able having the power to do something

*Franco is **able** to count to one hundred.*

aboard on a ship, bus, train, or airplane
*All **aboard**!*

about 1 just before or just after
*It's **about** four o'clock.*
2 having to do with
*This is a book **about** ships.*

above 1 overhead
*the sky **above***
2 higher than
*The bird flew **above** the trees.*

abrupt sudden
*an **abrupt** ending*

absent not here

accelerator one of the pedals in a car. The driver presses it with one foot to make the car go faster.

accent the way people say their words
*Australians have a different **accent** from Canadians.*

accept to take what is offered to you

accident 1 something bad that happens and is not meant to happen
2 by chance
*We met by **accident**.*

accompany 1 to go with someone
2 to play a musical instrument while someone sings or dances

account 1 a report about something that has happened **2** a list that tells you how much money you owe or have spent

accurate correct and exact

accuse to say that someone has done something wrong

ace a card used in games
*A deck of cards has four **aces** in it.*

ache to have a pain that goes on hurting
*My head is **aching**.*

achievement something difficult or special that you have done

acorn the nut of an oak tree

acrobat someone who does exciting jumping and balancing acts to entertain people

across from one side to the other
*I swam **across** the river.*

act 1 to take part in a play **2** to do something

action 1 a movement **2** something that is done

active busy or working

activity 1 being busy doing things **2** something for you to do

actor a man who acts in a play

actress a woman who acts in a play

actual real

add 1 to put together with something else
*Sally wants to **add** sugar to her cereal.*
2 to find the answer to a question like 3+3 = ?

adder a small snake

addition 1 adding numbers **2** something that is added
*We put an **addition** on our house.*

additional extra

address the number, street, town, and province where someone lives

adjective any word that tells you what someone or something is like.
*Beautiful, tall, old, hard, and green are all **adjectives**.*

admiral a very important officer in the navy

admire 1 to think someone or something is very good
2 to look at something and enjoy it
*They were **admiring** the view.*

admission letting someone in

admit 1 to let someone come in
2 to say you were the person who did something, when someone asks if you did it
*He **admitted** that he stole the jewels.*

adopt to take someone into your family.

adore to like very much

adult someone who is fully grown

advance to move forward

advantage something exciting that happens

adverb any word that tells you how, when, or where something happens.
*Away, often, somewhere, now, slowly, and quickly are all **adverbs**.*

advertisement (ad-ver-tis-ment)
words or pictures that try to make you buy something

advice something said to someone to help him decide what to do

advise to tell someone what you think would be best to do

affect to make someone different in some way

affection a feeling you have for someone or something you like a lot

afford to have enough money to pay for something

afraid in fear of

after 1 following
*Bill walked in **after** Sheila did.*
2 past the time of
*Mom went to sleep **after** dinner.*
3 in search of
*The dog chased **after** the children.*

afternoon the time from the middle of the day until about six o'clock

afterwards later

again once more
*Try **again**!*

against 1 on the opposite side to
*We played **against** your team and won.*
2 on or next to
*He leaned **against** the wall.*

age how old someone or something is

agent someone whose job is to arrange things for people
*a travel **agent***

agile able to move quickly and easily

ago in the past
The show started ten minutes ***ago***.

agree to think the same as someone else

aground trapped on sand or rocks in shallow water. Ships sometimes run aground on rocks and are badly damaged.

ahead in front
*I went on **ahead** to open the gate.*

aid 1 help
2 something that helps
*a hearing **aid***

aim 1 to point at something
***Aim** your finger.*
2 to try to do something
*They **aimed** at finishing the spelling test before lunch.*

air what everyone breathes

air conditioner a machine that cools or heats air

aircraft any airplane or helicopter

air force a group of people trained to use airplanes in war

airplane a flying machine with a motor and with wings that do not move

airport a place where people can go to get on or off airplanes

air-tight tightly closed so that air cannot get into it or out of it
*An **air-tight** jar*

aisle (sounds like tile)
a path between groups of seats. Churches and buses have aisles.

alarm 1 a sudden, frightened feeling
2 a warning sound or sign

album a book where you can keep things like stamps or photographs

alas a word showing sadness
***Alas** it is raining and we cannot go out.*

alert lively and ready for anything
*an **alert** policeman*

alike much the same

alive living

all 1 everyone or everything
*Let's start singing. **All** together now...*
2 the whole of something
*He's eaten **all** the cake.*

alley a very narrow street

alligator a large animal that lives in rivers. It has short legs, a long body, and sharp teeth.

allow to let something happen

all right 1 safe and well
2 I agree
***All right** you can stay up.*

ally a person or country that supports another
*Canada is an **ally** of Norway.*

almond a kind of flat nut with a very hard shell

almost very nearly
*We're **almost** home now.*

alone by yourself or by itself

along 1 from one end to the other
*He ran **along** the top of the wall.*
2 to go with, together
*Come **along!** Hurry Up!*

aloud in a voice that can be heard

alphabet all the letters in writing a language, arranged in order

already 1 by this time
*He was **already** there when we arrived.*
2 before now
*I've **already** done that.*

also as well
*cake and **also** ice cream*

altar a kind of table in the front of a church

alter to change

alteration a change in someone or something

although and yet or though
***Although** it was hot, she wore a fur coat.*

altogether counting everything or everyone
*There are twenty-nine in our class **altogether**.*

aluminum a very light metal, silver in colour

always at all times
*He's **always** hungry.*

am see **be**

amateur 1 someone who does something as a hobby
2 someone who takes part in a sport and is not paid

amaze to surprise greatly

ambition something that you want to do very much
*Her **ambition** is to be a doctor.*

ambulance a van for taking injured or ill people to hospital

ammunition anything that is fired from a gun

among in the middle of
*Your book must be somewhere **among** these books.*

amount how much or how many there are
*a large **amount** of money*

amuse 1 to make someone laugh or smile
2 to make time pass pleasantly for someone
*I was **amusing** myself with this puzzle.*

amusement something that makes you happy or pleased

an 1 one
*Did you eat **an** apple?*
2 one sort of
*The beaver is **an** animal.*
3 each, every
*The children rested once **an** hour.*

ancestor a member of the same family who lived long ago

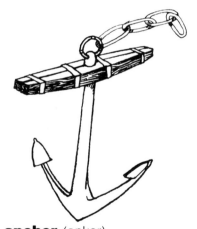

anchor (anker)
a heavy metal hook joined to a ship by a chain. It is dropped into the sea, where it digs into the bottom to hold the ship in place in the water.

ancient very old

anger a strong feeling that you get when you are not pleased. It makes you want to fight or hurt someone.

angle the corner where two lines meet

angler a fisherman who uses a rod, hook, and line

angry feeling anger

animal anything that lives and can move about. Birds, fish, snakes, wasps, and elephants are all animals.

ankle the thin part of the leg where it is joined to the foot

anniversary a day when you remember something special that happened on the same day in another year
*a wedding **anniversary***

announce to say something in front of a lot of people

annoy to make someone angry

annual happening every year
*Our school has an **annual** show.*

another 1 a different one
2 one more
*No, you can't have **another** candy.*

answer 1 to say something to someone who has asked you a question
2 something that is said or done in return

ant a tiny insect

Antarctic the very cold land in the south of the earth

antelope a kind of deer

antler a horn on the head of a deer or moose

antenna wires or metal rods for picking up or sending out radio and television waves

antique (an-teek) something valuable that is very old

anxious worried

any 1 one or some
*Have you **any** wool?*
2 at all
*Are you **any** better?*

anybody, anyone any person

anything any thing
*It's so dark, I can't see **anything**.*

anywhere in any place

apart away from each other
*Halifax and Vancouver are far **apart**.*

apartment a room or rooms in a building for people to live in

ape an animal like a large monkey with long arms and no tail. Chimpanzees and gorillas are apes.

apologize to say that you are sorry for doing something

apostrophe a punctuation mark (') to show ownership or to

11

stand for a missing letter
The teacher's book is red. It's big too.

apparatus special things that you use for doing something
The magician set up his apparatus to do a trick.

appeal to ask for something that you need
He appealed for help.

appear 1 to come and be seen
Just call and the dog will appear.
2 to seem
That man appears to be very sad.

appearance 1 what someone looks like
2 coming so that you can be seen
He made an appearance at the game.

appendix the small tube inside the body that sometimes causes an illness called appendicitis

appetite the wish for food

applaud to clap to show that you are pleased

applause clapping

apple a round juicy fruit that is white inside, and has a red, green or yellow skin

appoint to choose someone for a job

appointment a time when you have arranged to go and see someone
an appointment with the dentist

approach to come near to

approximate nearly correct

apricot a round, soft, juicy fruit. It has a large stone in it and thin, orange skin.

apron something worn over the front of the body to keep the clothes underneath clean

aquarium a large, glass container where fish are kept

arc part of the curved line of a circle

arch a curved part that helps to support a bridge or building

archery shooting at a target with a bow and arrow

architect (arkitect) someone whose job is to draw plans for buildings

Arctic the very cold sea and land in the north of the earth

are see **be**

area 1 an amount of surface
2 a part of a country or place
a no smoking area

arena a large covered building with a big flat surface inside for playing games like hockey

aren't a short form of are not

argue to talk about something with people who do not agree with you.

argument talking in an angry or excited way to someone who does not agree with you

arithmetic finding out about numbers

arm the part of the body between the shoulder and the hand

armchair a comfortable chair with parts at the side for you to rest your arms on

armour, armor 1 metal clothes worn in battles long ago
2 sheets of metal put round ships and tanks to protect them

armpit the part underneath the top of the arm

arms weapons

army a large group of people trained to fight on land

around 1 all round

Around the castle was a thick forest.
2 here and there
Look around for it.

arouse to wake someone up

arrange to put in order

arrangement something that has been arranged

arrest to take someone prisoner
The policeman arrested the thief.

arrive to come to the end of a journey

arrow 1 a pointed stick that is shot from a bow
2 a sign that points in a direction

arrowhead the pointed tip on the end of an arrow

art 1 drawing and painting
2 the ability to do something difficult
She has an art for writing

article a particular thing

artificial not natural because it has been made by people or machines
artificial flowers

artist someone who draws or paints pictures

as 1 equally
Can you play as well as Tony?
2 in the same way
Watch Nadia and do as she does.

13

3 at the same time
Billy looked up **as** *the pony came closer.*
4 because
We must work fast **as** *it is going to rain.*
5 though
Tall **as** *Cathy was, she could not reach the top.*

ascend (a-send)
to go up

ash 1 the gray powder left when something has been burned
2 a kind of tree

ashamed feeling very sorry and guilty about something

ashore on land
The sailors went **ashore**.

aside to one side
Stand **aside**.

ask to speak in order to find out or get something

asleep sleeping

ass a donkey

assembly the time when the whole school meets together

assist to help

assistance help

assistant someone whose job is to help someone else

assorted with different sorts put together

asteroid a small chunk of matter that moves around in space

astonish to surprise greatly

astonishment great surprise

astronaut someone who travels in space

astronomer someone who studies the stars and planets

astronomy finding out about the stars and planets

at 1 where
We are **at** *school.*
2 when
We sleep **at** *night.*
3 how
She ran **at** *a high speed.*
4 in what direction
He pointed **at** *the fence.*

ate see **eat**

athlete someone who trains to be good at sports

atlas a book of maps

atmosphere the air around the earth

atom one of the very tiny things that everthing is made up of

attach to join or fasten

attack to start fighting

attempt to try

attend 1 to be in a place in order to take part in something **2** to listen carefully

attendance being at a place in order to take part in something
school **attendance**

attention 1 careful listening, reading, or thinking
2 *pay* **attention** take notice

attic a room or rooms just under the roof of a house

attract 1 to interest
2 to make something come nearer

attractive very pleasant to look at

auction (oction)
a sale when things are sold to the people who offer the most money for them

audience people who have come to a place to see or hear something

audio-tape a long thin tape on which you can record sounds

aunt your uncle's wife or the sister of one of your parents

author someone who writes books or stories

authority the power to make other people do as you say

automatic able to work on its own and control itself. Some machines are automatic.

automobile a car

autumn the part of the year when leaves fall off the trees and it gets colder. It is also called the fall.

available ready for you to use or get

avalanche a large amount of snow, rock, or ice sliding suddenly down a mountain

avenue a road, often with trees along each side

average ordinary or usual
of **average** *height for his age*

avoid to keep out of the way of someone or something

await to wait for

awake not sleeping

award a prize

aware knowing about something

away 1 not here
She was **away** *yesterday.*
2 to another place
He ran **away**.

awful very bad

awhile for a time

*The wolf rested **awhile** under the bush.*

awkward clumsy
2 not convenient
*an **awkward** time*

axe a tool for chopping

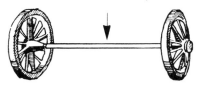

axle a rod that goes through the centre of wheels to join them

baby a very young child

baby sitter a person who takes care of a child when its parents are away

bachelor a man who has not married

back 1 the side opposite the front
2 the part of the body between the neck and the waist

backward, backwards
1 with the first part last, or the front at the back
2 toward the rear
3 slow in learning

bad 1 wicked or evil
*Stealing is **bad**.*
2 harmful
*Too much rain will be **bad** for the wheat.*
3 in poor condition
*Dad has a **bad** back.*
4 serious
*There was a **bad** fire in Ottawa last night.*

badge something worn pinned or stitched to clothes. It shows which group someone belongs to.
*a school **badge**, a sheriff's **badge***

bag a container such as a purse or a suitcase or a sack made of paper

baggage luggage

bail to throw water out of a boat

bait food put on a hook or in a trap to catch fish and other animals

bake to cook inside an oven

baker someone whose job is to make or sell bread and pastry

balance 1 what is left over after subtracting
*Three from six leaves a **balance** of three.*

2 to keep something steady
The beaver **balanced** *the branch in its mouth.*

balcony 1 a platform with a rail around it outside an upstairs window
2 the seats upstairs in a theatre

bald without any hair on the head

bale 1 a large bundle or package
a **bale** *of hay*
2 *to* **bale out** to jump out of an airplane with a parachute

ball 1 a round object used in games
2 a big party with a lot of dancing

ballad a song or poem that tells a story
Verna sang a **ballad** *about Louis Riel.*

ballerina a woman who is a ballet-dancer

ballet a story told on the stage in dancing, mime, and music

balloon 1 a small, coloured, rubber bag that you can blow up
2 a bag filled with hot air or gas so that it floats in the sky

bamboo a tall plant with stiff, hollow stems. It grows in very hot countries.

banana a long fruit with a thick

yellow skin

band 1 a group of people
2 some people playing musical instruments together
3 a strip of material. Bands are put around things to decorate them or to keep them together.
a rubber **band**

bandage a strip of material for wrapping around part of the body that has been hurt

bandit a person who is a robber

bang 1 the sudden, loud, hard sound an explosion makes
2 to hit or shut with a loud noise
Don't **bang** *the door!*

banish to send someone away from a place as a punishment
also **ban**

banjo a musical instrument with strings that you play with your fingers. It is smaller and rounder than a guitar.

bank 1 a place that looks after

money and valuable things for people

2 the ground near the edge of a river, canal, or lake

3 a large amount of sand or earth piled up

banner a kind of flag

banquet (*bank*wet) a big feast given by someone

bar 1 a long piece of wood or metal

2 a block of chocolate, toffee, or soap

3 a place that serves food and drinks at a counter

*a coffee **bar***

barbecue 1 a picnic outdoors

2 an outdoor fireplace for cooking food

3 to cook food over an open fire

barbed wire wire with sharp spikes in it, used for making fences

barber a person whose job is to cut hair

bare without any clothes or covering

barge a long boat with a flat bottom. Barges are used on canals.

bark 1 to make the sound a dog makes

2 the hard covering around a tree's trunk and branches

barge

barley a grain grown by farmers

barn a large building on a farm, where things are kept

barracks an army building where soldiers live together

barren without any plants or trees

barrier something that stands in the way

base the bottom part of something

baseball 1 a game played with a bat and ball

2 the ball used in the game of baseball

basement the rooms in a building that are below the ground

bashful shy

BASIC a language for programming computers. BASIC stands for Beginner's All-Purpose Symbolic Instruction Code.

basin a bowl

basket a container made of straw or cane

basketball 1 a game in which players try to put a ball through hoops
2 the large round ball used in basketball

bat 1 an animal like a mouse with wings
2 a piece of wood for hitting a ball in a game

batch a number of things together
*a **batch** of letters*

bath 1 a washing of the body
*Mom said I have to have a **bath**.*
2 the large tub which holds water for a bath
3 a bathroom

bathroom the room where you can have a bath or wash

batter 1 a mixture made from flour, egg, and milk. It is used for making pancakes and frying fish.
2 to damage something by hitting it often

*The wind **battered** down the fence.*

battery a closed container with electricity inside it. You put batteries inside things like radios to make them work.

battle fighting between groups of people

bawl to shout or cry loudly

bay a place where the shore bends inwards and the sea fills the space

bayonet a sharp blade that can be fixed to a gun

be 1 to exist or occur
*How can that **be**?*
2 to have or show a certain quality
*Will Steve **be** upset?*
(**be** has many forms, such as *am, are, is, was, were, been, being*)
*I **am** coming.*
*They **are** here.*
*Millie **is** absent.*
*Jack **was** absent yesterday.*
*Frank and Tina **were** absent on Thursday.*

*Cathy has **been** away all week. Our class is **being** taken on a trip.*

beach land by the edge of the water. It is usually covered with sand or small stones.

beacon a light or fire that warns of danger

bead a small, round object

beak the hard part around a bird's mouth

beam 1 a long piece of wood
2 a line of light
3 to smile very happily

bean a vegetable. Beans are round seeds and some sorts grow inside long green pods that can also be eaten.

beanbag a small cloth bag filled with dried beans, used in games

bear 1 to put up with
*He cannot **bear** any more pain. He has already **borne** too much.*
2 to give birth to
*The baby was **born** yesterday.*
3 a large animal with very thick fur

beard hair growing on a man's face

beast any big animal

beat 1 to do better than someone else

*You **beat** me last time.*
2 to hit often
***Beat** the rug until the dust is gone.*
3 to stir very hard

beautiful 1 very attractive
*a **beautiful** face*
2 very pleasant
*a **beautiful** day*

beauty something or someone beautiful

beaver a land and water animal with thick fur and a flat tail
***Beavers** are found all over Canada.*

Beaver a young Boy Scout. see **Boy Scout**

became see **become**

because for the reason that
*I got wet **because** it rained.*

beckon to move your hand to show someone that you want him to come nearer

become to come to be
*It suddenly **became** very cold yesterday.*

bed 1 a piece of furniture to sleep on
2 a piece of ground where plants are grown

bee an insect that can fly, sting, and make honey

beech a kind of tree

beef meat from an ox, bull, or cow.

beehive a kind of box for keeping bees

beetle a flying insect that can put hard covers over its wings

before 1 earlier than
*I was here **before** you.*
2 in front of
*It vanished **before** my eyes.*

began see **begin**

beggar someone who lives by asking other people for money, clothes, or food

begin to start
*The game will **begin** now.*
*I'm **beginning** to understand.*
*He **began** school last week.*
*I have **begun** piano lessons.*

beginner someone who has just started learning something

beginning the start of something

begun see begin

behave to show good or bad manners in front of other people

behind at the back of
*He hid **behind** the wall.*

beige a colour that is very light brown

belief what someone believes

believe to feel sure that something is true.

bell a hollow piece of metal that rings when it is hit

belong 1 to be someone's
*That pen **belongs** to me.*
2 to be part of something
*Dave **belongs** to the Boy Scouts.*
3 to be in the proper place
*The hammer **belongs** in the tool box*

below underneath
*Write your address **below** your name.*

belt a band worn around the waist

bench a seat for more than one person

bend 1 to make something curved or not straight
2 to lean over so that your head is nearer to the ground
*He **bent** down and looked at his shoes.*

beneath underneath

bent see bend

berry any small, round fruit with seeds in it

beside at the side of

a house **beside** *the sea*

besides as well as
ten people **besides** *me*

best better than any other
my **best** *friend*

better superior in quality
She is **better** *than I am in swimming.*

between **1** in the middle of two people or things
I sat **between** *Mom and Dad.*
2 something that is shared
Mike and Sheila have a dime **between** *them.*

beware be careful

bewildered very puzzled

bewitched under a spell

beyond further than
Don't go **beyond** *the end of the road.*

bicycle, bike a machine with two wheels and pedals that you can ride

big large in size or amount

bill **1** a piece of paper that tells you how much money you owe
2 a bird's beak

bind to tie together

binoculars a special pair of glasses like two tubes joined together. When you look through them, things far away seem much nearer.

birch a tree with white bark

bird any animal with feathers, wings, and a beak

birth the beginning of life, when a baby leaves its mother and starts to breathe

birthday the date each year when you remember the day someone was born

biscuit a kind of small, thin, dry cake or bread

bishop a priest who is in charge of other priests

bison a wild ox-like creature found in North America. It is often incorrectly called a buffalo.   see **buffalo**

bit **1** a very small amount of something
2 a small piece of information that can be put into a computer see **byte**
3 the part of a bridle that goes into a horse's mouth
4 see **bite**

bite to use the teeth to cut into something
Your dog's **bitten** *me.*
Stop **biting** *your nails!*
She **bit** *into the apple pie.*

bitter not sweet

black a colour

blackberry a small, soft, black berry that grows on bushes

blackbird one of a family of medium-sized birds, usually black

blackboard a surface that you can write on with chalk

blackfly a black biting insect found largely in northern Canada

blacksmith someone whose job is to make horseshoes and other things out of iron

blade 1 the flat, sharp part of a knife or sword
2 something shaped like a blade
a **blade** of grass

blame to say that it is because of a certain person or thing that something bad has happened

blank an empty space with nothing written or drawn on it

blanket a thick cover used on a bed

blast 1 sudden, rushing wind or air
2 to blow up

blaze 1 to burn brightly
2 to show the way

The trapper **blazed** a trail for his friends.

blazer a kind of jacket. A blazer usually has a badge on its top pocket.

bleach to make something white

bleak cold, miserable, and windy
a **bleak** day

bleat to make the sound sheep make

bleed to lose blood
His nose **bled** for ten minutes.

blend to mix together

blew see **blow**

blind 1 not able to see
2 a screen that you pull down to cover a window

blink to close your eyes and open them again very quickly

blister a small swelling on the skin. It has liquid inside and hurts when you touch it.

blizzard a storm with a lot of snow and wind

block 1 a thick piece of something solid like wood or stone
2 to be in the way so that something cannot get through

blond, blonde with light hair

blood a red liquid that moves around inside the body

a **b** c d e f g h i j k l m n o p q r s t u v w x y z

bloom to be in flower
*Roses **bloom** in summer.*

blossom flowers on a tree

blot a spot or stain on something

blouse a piece of clothing worn on the top half of the body

blow 1 to make air come out of the mouth
*She **blew** out the candles and cut the cake.*
2 to move along with the wind
*Shingles were **blown** off the roof.*

blue a colour

blueberry a small dark-blue fruit

blue jay a blue and white and gray bird with a crest of feathers on the top of its head
***Blue jays** are very noisy.*

blunt not sharp
*a **blunt** knife*

blur to make something look not clear. Smudged writing is blurred.

blush to go red in the face because you feel shy or guilty

board 1 a long piece of thin wood
2 stiff cardboard
3 to get on an airplane, bus, ship, or train

boast 1 to talk in a way that shows you are much too proud

of yourself and what you can do. Boast means the same as brag.

boat something that floats and has room in it for taking people or things over water

bobcat a wild cat slightly larger than a house cat

bob white a brown and white bird that makes a call which sounds like its name

body all of a person or animal that can be seen or touched

bodyguard a person or persons whose job is to protect someone

bog any place that stays wet for most of the year. Swamps and marshes are often called bogs.

boil 1 to heat liquid until it bubbles
2 to cook something in hot, bubbling water
3 a big painful spot on the skin

boiler a large container in which water is heated

bold brave and not afraid

bolt 1 to rush off
2 a kind of sliding fastener used on doors
3 a thick metal pin like a screw

bomb a weapon that blows up and does a lot of damage

bone any of the separate parts of a skeleton

24

bonfire a large fire built in the open air

book 1 sheets of paper fastened together and fixed to a cover **2** to arrange for a seat to be kept for you

bookcase a piece of furniture made for holding books

boom to make a loud, deep sound
*The guns **boomed** away in the distance.*

boomerang a curved stick that comes back to the person who throws it

boot a kind of shoe that also covers the ankle

border 1 the narrow part along the edge of something
*a **border** of flowers*
2 the line where two countries meet
*The **border** between Canada and the U.S.A. is one of the longest in the world.*

bore 1 to make someone tired by being dull

*a **boring** film*
2 to make a hole with a tool

born, borne see **bear**

borrow to get the use of something for a short time and agree to give it back

both the two of them
*He took **both** of the cakes.*

bother to worry or annoy someone

bottom 1 the lowest part of anything
2 the part of the body that you sit on

bough a large branch

bought see buy

boulder a large, smooth rock

bounce to spring back after hitting something

bound 1 to leap
2 see **bind**

boundary a line marking the edge of some land

bouquet (boo-kay) a bunch of flowers

bow[1] (rhymes with go)
1 a strip of bent wood with string joined to each end, for shooting arrows
2 a wooden rod with strong hairs stretched along it and joined to each end, for playing the violin
3 a knot with loops

25

bow[2] (rhymes with cow)
to bend forwards to show
respect
*He **bowed** to the
Governor-General.*

bowl (bole)
a round, open container for
liquid or food

bowling a game in which you
roll balls at large wooden pins to
knock them down

box 1 a container with a lid
*a cardboard **box***
2 to fight with the fists

boxcar a railroad car that can
be closed on all sides and the
top
*The **boxcar** was loaded with
wheat from Saskatchewan.*

boy a male child or teenager

Boy Scout a member of a
world-wide organization that
encourages boys to be good
citizens

bracket 1 a piece of metal fixed
to a wall to support something
2 one of a pair of marks like
these ( )

brain the part inside the top of
the head that controls the body.
It also makes people able to
think and remember.

brake the part of a car or bicycle
that makes it slow down or stop

branch a part that sticks out

from the trunk of a tree

brand 1 a mark to show the
maker or owner
2 a certain kind of goods
*a new **brand** of tea*

brass a yellow metal made by
mixing copper with other metals

brave ready and able to bear
pain or danger

bravery the ability to do brave
deeds

bread a food made by baking
dough in loaves

break 1 to snap, smash, or
crack
*The cup **broke** when I dropped
it.*
2 to fail to keep a law or
promise
*He's **broken** the rules.*
3 a short rest from work

breakfast the first meal of the
day

breath the air that a person
breaths

breathe to take air into your
lungs through your nose or
mouth and send it out again

breed a certain kind of animal
*Holsteins are a common **breed**
of cow in Canada.*

breeze a gentle wind

brick a small, oblong block used
in building

bride a woman on the day she gets married

bridegroom a man on the day he gets married

bridesmaid a girl or woman who helps the bride at her wedding

bridge something built to go over a river, railway, or a road

brief short
a **brief** talk

bright 1 shining
a **bright** star
2 intelligent
a **bright** boy
3 cheerful
a **bright** smile

brilliant very bright

bring 1 to carry here
Bring your book
2 to lead here
Yesterday he **brought** his friend.

brink the edge of a dangerous place

brisk quick and lively

bristle a short, stiff hair like the hairs on a brush

brittle likely to break or snap

broad measuring a lot from side to side
a **broad** river

broadcast a television or radio program

broke, broken see **break**

bronze a brown metal made by mixing copper and tin

brook a small stream

broom a stiff brush for sweeping, with a long handle

broth a thin soup made from meat and vegetables

brother a man or boy who has the same parents as another person

brought see **bring**

brow 1 the forehead
2 the top of a hill

brown a colour

Brownie a young Girl Guide

bruise a mark that comes on the skin when it has been hit hard

brush a tool with short, stiff hairs. Brushes are used for making hair tidy, cleaning, sweeping, scrubbing, and painting.

bubble 1 a small ball of air inside liquid
2 to be full of bubbles

buck 1 a male deer, hare, or rabbit
2 to leap like a horse about to throw someone off its back

bucket a container with a handle used for carrying liquid

buckle a kind of fastening used on belts or straps

bud a flower or leaf before it has opened

budge to move slightly
I've pushed hard but it won't
budge.

buffalo a kind of wild ox found in Africa and Asia
see **bison**

buffet (buffay)
a piece of furniture used for storing dishes

bug 1 any kind of insect or creature with many legs
2 a mistake in a computer program

bugle a small brass musical instrument that you blow

build to make something by putting things carefully on top of one another
*Last autumn we **built** a huge bonfire.*

building something that has been built. Houses, schools, theatres, stores and churches are all buildings.

built see **build**

bulb 1 a glass electric lamp
2 something that looks like an onion and is planted in soil. Daffodils, tulips, and some other flowers grow from bulbs.

bulge to swell out

bulk a large amount

bull a male animal such as moose, elk, or elephant

bulldozer a heavy machine for clearing land

bullet a small lump of metal made to be fired from a gun

bullfrog a large frog

bully someone who attacks or threatens a weaker person

bulrush a tall plant that grows near water

bumblebee a large bee with a loud buzz

bump 1 to knock against something by accident
*The giant **bumped** his head on the ceiling.*
2 a swelling

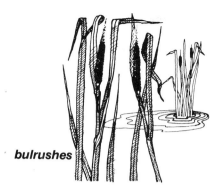

bulrushes

bumper a bar along the front or back of a car

bumpy rough, not smooth

bunch a group of things joined or tied together
a **bunch** of bananas

bundle a group of things tied together

bungalow a house without any upstairs rooms

bunk a bed that has another bed above or below it

bunny a rabbit

buoy (boy)
something that floats on the water, but is fixed to one spot to guide ships

burden something that has to be carried

burglar someone who gets into a building to steal things

burial (berrial)

the burying of a dead person see **bury**

burn 1 to hurt or damage something with fire or heat
2 to be on fire

burrow a hole in the ground that an animal lives in

burst to break open suddenly
*The balloon **burst** when I blew it up.*

bury to put something in a hole in the ground and cover it over

bus a kind of big car with a lot of seats, that people can travel in

bush a plant that looks like a small tree
2 a wilderness area

business (biznis)
1 a person's work
2 a store of firm

bustle to hurry in a busy or fussy way

busy 1 doing things all the time
2 full of activity
a **busy** street

but 1 except
*Every province **but** two agreed to the new law.*
2 on the other hand
*Julie is short **but** she is quick.*
3 only
*The farm had **but** one horse.*

butcher someone who cuts up meat and sells it

29

butter a yellow food made from cream. It is spread on bread and biscuits.

buttercup a wild flower with shiny yellow petals

butterfly an insect with large white or coloured wings

butterscotch hard candy made from sugar and butter

button a fastener sewn on clothes. It fits into a hole or loop.

buy to get something by giving money for it
*I **bought** this bike from him yesterday.*

buzz to make the sound a bee makes

by 1 next to, near
*The tree is **by** a stream.*
2 by means of
*The family came **by** boat.*
3 not later than
*We will be in Winnipeg **by** Tuesday.*

4 during
*Owls sleep **by** day.*

byte a group of bits in a computer that is treated as one unit
see **bit 2**

Cc

cab 1 the part of a truck, bus, or train where the driver sits
2 a taxi

cabbage a round vegetable with a lot of green leaves

cabin 1 a small house often made of logs
*The early pioneers lived in **cabins**.*
2 a room in a ship

cabinet a kind of cupboard with drawers

cable strong, thick wire or rope

cackle the sound a hen makes

cactus a plant with a thick green stem and thick green branches, covered in prickles. Cacti grow in hot, dry places and do not need much water.

cafe (kaffay)
a place where you can buy a drink, a snack, or a meal

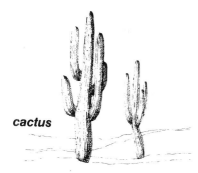

cactus

cafeteria a kind of cafe where you get your own food from the counter

cage a large box with bars

cake a food made with flour, butter, eggs, and sugar
fruit **cake**, *chocolate* **cake**

calamity something very bad that happens suddenly

calculator a machine that can do arithmetic

calendar a chart showing all the days, weeks, and months in a year

calf 1 the back part of the leg between the knee and the ankle **2** the young of such animals as cows, moose, and elephants

call 1 to speak loudly
2 to give a name to someone or something
3 to tell someone to come to you

calm 1 still

a **calm** *sea*
2 not noisy or excited

calves more than one calf

came see **come**

camel a big animal with one or two humps on its back. Camels are used instead of horses in deserts, because they can travel for a long time without eating or drinking.

camera a kind of box that you put a film in and use for taking photographs

camouflage (*cam*-oh-flahj) to hide something by making it look like other things that are near it. Most wild animals are camouflaged by their colour or shape, when they are not moving.

camp a place where people take vacations in the outdoors
People who go **camping** *often stay in tents.*

can 1 to be able to
Betty **can** *play hockey but Dorothy* **can't**.
Billy **could** *skate when he was four years old but I* **couldn't**.
2 a round metal container

Canada the largest and most northern country in North America

Canada goose a wild water bird found all over Canada. It has a black neck with a white patch at the throat.

Canadian 1 a citizen of Canada
2 about Canada or the people who live there

canal a kind of river made by people, so that boats can go directly from one place to another

canary a small yellow bird that sings

candle a stick of wax with string through the centre. It gives light as it burns.

candlestick something that holds a candle

candy a sweet food made mostly of sugar

cane 1 the hard stem of some plants
2 a long, thin stick

cannon a big gun that fires heavy metal balls

canoe (ca-*noo*)
a light, narrow boat that you move by using a paddle

canter one of the ways a horse can move. It is faster than a trot but slower than a gallop.

canoe

canvas strong material for making things like tents

cap 1 a small hat
2 a top or covering

capable able to do something
*You're **capable** of better work.*

capacity the largest amount a container can hold

cape a short cloak

capital 1 the most important city in a country or province
*Halifax is the **capital** of Nova Scotia.*
2 one of the big letters put at the beginning of names and sentences. A,B,C,D, and so on are capital letters.

capsule 1 a very small container usually full of medicine
2 a separate part at the front of a space ship. It can move on its own away from the main part.

captain 1 an officer in the army or navy
2 someone who is in charge of a team

captive a person or animal

that has been captured

capture 1 to take prisoner
2 to get something by fighting for it

car 1 an automobile
2 a large vehicle for people to ride in
a railroad car

card 1 a piece of heavy paper with a picture and a message on it. You send cards to people at special times like birthdays.
2 one of a set of small pieces of cardboard with numbers or pictures on them, used in games.

cardboard very thick, strong paper
a cardboard box

cardigan a kind of knitted jacket or sweater

care 1 worry or trouble
2 to take care of to look after
3 to care for to look after
4 to care about to be very interested in something

careful making sure that you do things safely and well
a careful driver

careless not careful

caretaker someone whose job is to look after a building

cargo things taken by ship or airplane from one place to another

cargoes of fruit

carnation a garden plant with white, pink, or red flowers that smell very sweet

carnival 1 a gay procession with people wearing fancy dress
2 a festival
see **fair**

carol a happy song sung at Christmas

carpenter someone whose job is to make things out of wood

carpet a thick cover for the floor

carrot an orange vegetable shaped like a cone

carry to take people, animals, or things from one place to another

cart a kind of box on wheels

carton a light container made of cardboard or plastic

cartoon 1 a film that uses drawings instead of actors
2 a drawing that tells a joke

cartridge a small container with a bullet and an explosive inside

carve 1 to cut something hard into a shape
2 to cut off slices of meat

cascade a waterfall

case 1 a container
a pencil case
2 a suitcase

33

cash coins or paper money

casserole food baked in a large, deep dish
*Chris made a tuna **casserole**.*

cassette 1 a small closed container with a reel of tape inside it for recording sounds, or playing back sounds
2 as in **1**, but for information to be used in a computer

cast 1 a shape made by pouring liquid metal or plaster into a mould
2 all the actors in a play
3 to throw
*He **cast** his net into the sea to catch fish.*

castaway someone who has been shipwrecked

castle a large, strong house with very thick, stone walls

cat a small furry animal usually kept as a pet
*Our house **cat** is named Muffin.*

catalogue a list

catch 1 to capture
2 to get hold of something
3 to get an illness
*I **caught** a cold last week.*

caterpillar a long, creeping creature that will turn into a butterfly or moth

cathedral a big, important church

cattle cows and bulls kept by a farmer

caught see **catch**

cauldron a large pot used for cooking
*a witch's **cauldron***

cauliflower a vegetable with a thick white stalk covered in small, hard, white flowers

cause to make something happen

cautious only doing what is safe
*a **cautious** man*

cave a big hole under the ground or inside a mountain

cavern a large cave

cease to stop doing something

ceiling the flat part that covers the top of a room

celebrate to do special things to show you are very happy about something

celebration a party for something special

celery a vegetable with white stalks that can be eaten raw

cell one of the small rooms where prisoners are kept in a prison

cellar a room underneath the building. Cellars are used for storing things.

celsius a way of measuring temperature that gives 0 degrees for freezing water and 100 degrees for boiling water

cement a mixture of clay and lime used in building to stick things together

cemetery (*sem*-e-tair-ee) a place where dead people are buried

cent money
*A penny is worth one **cent**.*

centimetre, centimeter a measure for length
*My ruler is thirty **centimetres** long.*

centipede a long, creeping creature with a lot of tiny legs

centre, center the point or part in the middle

century a hundred years

cereal 1 any plant grown by farmers for its seed
2 a food made from the seed of cereal plants and eaten at breakfast with milk

ceremony (serimony) something important and serious that is done in front of other people
*a marriage **ceremony***

certain 1 sure
*Are you **certain**?*
2 one in particular
*a **certain** person*

certificate a piece of paper that says you have done something special

chain 1 a line made of metal rings fastened together
2 a group of stores that have the same name, but are built in different places

chair a seat for one person

chalet (shallay) a small, wooden house with a large roof

chalk 1 a kind of soft white rock
2 a soft white stick used for writing on blackboards

chalkboard see **blackboard**

challenge to ask someone to try to do better than you at something

champion 1 someone who is the best in a sport
2 someone or something that wins a competition

championship a competition to decide on the champion

chance 1 a time when you can do something that you cannot do at other times
*This is your last **chance**.*
2 the way things happen that have not been planned
*I saw him by **chance** on the bus.*

change 1 to make or become different
2 to give something and get something in return
3 the money that you get back when you give more money that is needed to pay for something

chapel a kind of church

chapter a part of a book

character 1 someone in a story
2 the sort of person you are

charge 1 to ask a certain price
2 to buy something now and agree to pay for it later
3 to rush at something to attack it
4 in charge with the job of telling other people what they should do or how they should do it

chariot a kind of cart with two wheels, pulled by horses. Chariots were used long ago for fighting and racing.

chariot

charity gifts of money or help to people who need it

charm 1 a magic spell
2 a small ornament worn to bring good luck
3 the ability to make others feel good

chart 1 a big map
2 a large sheet of paper with information on it

chase to run after and try to catch a person or animal

chat to talk in a friendly way about things that are not important

chatter 1 to talk a lot or very quickly
2 to make a rattling noise
*His teeth **chattered** with fear.*

chauffeur (show-fur) someone whose job is to drive another person's car

cheap costing a small amount

cheat 1 to make another person believe what is not true so that

you can get something from her
2 to try to do well in a test or
game by breaking the rules

check 1 to go over something to
be sure it is correct or proper
Aunt Emily **checked** *the road
for broken glass.*
2 a piece of paper used instead
of cash
Mom paid for the bicycle by
check.
3 a bill for food or drink in a
restaurant.
4 a mark to show something is
correct, or has been looked at
The children put **checks** *on the
work that was finished.*

cheek the side of the face below
the eye

cheer to shout to show you are
pleased or that you want your
team to win

cheerful looking or sounding
happy
a **cheerful** *face*

cheese solid food with a strong
flavour, made from milk

cheque see **check 2**

chest 1 a big, strong box
2 the front part of the body
between the neck and the waist

chestnut 1 a large tree with
spreading branches
2 the shiny brown nut that
grows on a chestnut tree

chew to keep biting food while
you eat it

chicken a young bird kept for its
meat and eggs

chicken-pox an illness that
gives you red spots that itch

chief 1 the most important
2 the person in charge

child 1 a young boy or girl
2 a son or daughter
two **children**

chili a food made with meat, hot
pepper, and beans

chill 1 a bad cold that makes
you feel hot and dizzy
2 to make something cold

chime to make a tune like
church bells

chimney a tall pipe inside the
wall of a house. Smoke from the
fire moves up the chimney so
that it can get out through the
roof.

chimpanzee an African animal
like a large monkey with long
arms and no tail

chin the part of the face that is
under the mouth

china cups, saucers, and plates
made of very thin delicate
pottery

chip 1 a small piece of potato
that is fried

2 a very small piece of material in a computer, on which electrical information can be stored
3 to break or knock small pieces off something
a **chipped** vase

chipmunk a small animal with black and white stripes on its back

chisel a tool with a short, sharp edge, for cutting stone or wood

chocolate sweet food made from cocoa and sugar

choice 1 the chance to pick something
2 what you have picked
see **choose**

choir (kwire)
a group of people who sing together

choke 1 to find it hard to get your breath because of something in your throat.
The smoke made him **choke**.
2 to block up something
The pond was **choked** with weeds.

choose to take one thing instead of another, because you want to

Which car did you **choose**? Last time you **chose** a small one. What have you **chosen** this time?

chop 1 to cut something with a knife or axe
2 a small, thick slice of pork, lamb, or mutton

chopsticks a pair of thin sticks that may be used to eat with, instead of a knife and fork

chorus (kor-uss)
the words repeated after every verse in a poem or song

chose, chosen see **choose**

chrome, chromium (krome, krome-ium)
a bright, shiny metal that looks like silver

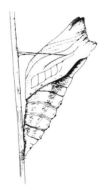

chrysalis (kriss-a-liss)
the cover a caterpillar makes around itself before it changes into a butterfly or moth

chuckle to laugh to yourself

chunk a thick lump
a **chunk** of meat

church a building where people worship

churn 1 a large container for milk
2 a machine for turning milk into butter

circle 1 the shape of a coin or wheel. The edge of a circle is always the same distance from the centre.
2 the curved line around the edge of a circle

circular like a circle

circus a show held in a big tent or building with animals, acrobats, and clowns

citizen a person who belongs to a country

city a big town

clad dressed

claim to ask for something that belongs to you

clap to make a noise by hitting the palm of one hand with the palm of the other

clash 1 to disagree with someone
2 to make the sound cymbals make

clasp to hold tightly

class a group of pupils who learn things together

claw one of the hard, sharp nails that some animals have on their feet

clay a sticky kind of earth used for making things, because it keeps its shape and goes hard

clean 1 free of dirt
a **clean** face
2 to make something free of dirt

clear 1 easy to understand, see, or hear
a **clear** photograph, a **clear** voice
2 free from things you do not want
a **clear** road, a **clear** day
3 to make something clear
Please **clear** the table.

clench to close your teeth, fingers, or fist tightly

clerk 1 a salesperson in a store
2 someone who sorts out papers and writes letters in an office

clever able to learn and understand things easily

cliff a steep rock close to the sea

climate the sort of weather that a place usually gets at different times of the year

climb to go up or down something high

cliff

clog

cling to hold tightly on to someone or something
*The child was afraid and **clung** to its mother.*

clinic a kind of hospital

clip 1 to cut something with scissors or a tool like scissors
*He **clipped** the hedge.*
2 a fastener for keeping things together or in place
*a paper **clip***

cloak a very loose coat without sleeves

cloakroom the room where you hang your coat

clock a machine that shows you what time it is

clockwise in the direction a clock's hands move

clog a kind of shoe with a wooden sole

close[1] (rhymes with dose)
1 very near
***close** to the fire*
2 careful
*a **close** look*
3 a street closed at one end

close[2] (rhymes with doze)
1 to shut
*The stores are **closing** early today.*
2 to end

cloth 1 material for making things like clothes and curtains
2 a piece of cloth for cleaning or covering something

clothes, clothing things worn to cover the body

cloud 1 something white, gray, or black that floats in the sky. Clouds are made of drops of water that often fall as rain.
2 dust or smoke that looks like a cloud

clover a green plant with red, white, or yellow flowers, found in lawns or used for hay

clown someone in a circus who wears funny clothes and make-up and makes people laugh

club 1 a group of people who meet together because they are interested in the same thing

2 a thick stick used as a weapon

3 a black clover leaf printed on some playing cards

clover

clue something that helps you to find the answer to a puzzle

clump a group of trees or plants growing close together

clumsy likely to knock things over or drop things

clung see **cling**

cluster 1 a group of things growing together
2 a group of people, animals, or things gathered around something

clutch 1 to snatch at something
2 to hold tightly

coach 1 a bus that takes people on long journeys
2 one of the separate parts of a train, where people sit
3 a kind of box on wheels pulled by several horses, that people can travel in

coal hard, black stuff that is burned to make heat

coarse not delicate or smooth. *Sacks are made of **coarse** material.*

coast the edge of land next to the sea

coat a piece of clothing with long sleeves that people wear over other clothes

cobweb a thin, sticky net spun by a spider to trap insects

cock a male bird

cocoa a brown powder used to make a hot drink that tastes of chocolate

coconut a big, round, hard seed that grows on palm trees. It has a sweet white food and liquid inside.

cod a large sea fish

code 1 a set of signs or letters for sending messages secretly or quickly
2 a set of rules

coffee a hot drink. It is made from cooked seeds crushed into a brown powder

coffin the long box in which a dead person is put

coil to wind rope or wire into rings

coin a piece of metal money

cold 1 how ice or snow feels
2 an illness that makes you
sneeze and blow your nose a
lot

collage (col-*ahj*)
a picture made from small
pieces of paper and material

collapse 1 to fall to pieces
2 to fall down because you are
ill

collar 1 the part that goes
around the neck of clothes
such as shirts and jackets
2 a band put around the neck
of a dog or cat

collect 1 to bring things
together from different places
They **collect** *foreign coins.*
2 to go and get someone or
something

collection a set of things that
have been collected
a stamp **collection**

collector someone who
collects things as a hobby or as
a job

college a school for people after
high school

collide to hit someone or
something by accident while
you are moving

collie a large, long-haired dog

collision a crash between two
moving things

colour, color 1 red, yellow, and
blue are examples of colours
2 to use paint or crayon on
something

colt a young, male horse

column 1 a list of numbers or
short lines of words, each below
the one that comes before it
2 a thick stone post that
supports something or
decorates a building
3 a special section of a
newspaper

comb 1 a strip of plastic, wood,
or metal with a row of thin parts
like teeth, for making hair tidy
2 to search a place very
carefully

combine 1 to join or mix
together
2 a special machine for
farmers to cut grain and
separate the seeds from the
straw

come 1 to move here
I **came** *as soon as I could.*
2 to arrive
Has the letter **come** *yet?*
It's **coming** *soon.*

comedian someone who
entertains people by making
them laugh

comedy a funny play

comfortable 1 pleasant to be
in, to sit on, or to wear
a **comfortable** *chair*
2 free from pain or worry

comic 1 funny
2 a paper with stories told in pictures

comma a punctuation mark (,) to divide parts of a sentence

command 1 to tell someone to do something
2 to be in charge of something

common usual, happening often
a **common** illness

commotion a lot of noise

communication 1 a message
2 a way of sending or getting a message

community the people living in one place

companion a friend who is with you

company 1 having another person or pet with you so that you are not lonely
The cat kept him **company**.
2 a group of people who do things together
a **company** of actors

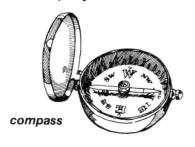
compass

compare to see how like each other some things are

compass an instrument that always shows where north is

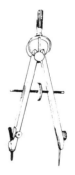

compasses an instrument for drawing circles
a pair of **compasses**

compete to take part in a race or competition

competition a kind of test or game with a prize for the person who wins

complain to say that you are not pleased about something

complete 1 whole
2 to come to the end of doing something

complicated 1 with a lot of different parts
a **complicated** machine
2 difficult
a **complicated** question

compliment words that praise

the person you are speaking to or writing to

composer someone who writes music

composition a story you have made up and written down

compound 1 a word made up of two or more words.
The word 'someone' is a **compound** *word.*
2 something made up of two or more things.
Concrete is a **compound** *of gravel, sand, and cement.*

computer a machine that can work things out very quickly, if it is given the right instructions and information

computer program the instructions that tell a computer what to do

conceal to hide

conceited too proud of yourself and what you can do

concentrate to think hard about one thing

concern 1 to be important or interesting to someone or something
2 worried

concert an entertainment with music

concrete a mixture of cement, gravel, and sand used for

making buildings, paths, and bridges

condense to make something smaller. Condensed milk is thicker than ordinary milk and takes up less space.

condition the state something is in

conductor 1 someone who looks after the passengers on a train
2 someone who stands facing a band, choir, or orchestra and keeps everyone playing together

cone a shape that is round at one end and pointed at the other

confess to say that you have done wrong

confetti tiny pieces of coloured paper that are thrown over a bride and bridegroom at a wedding

confident 1 brave and not afraid
a **confident** *swimmer*
2 sure about something

confuse to mix up

congratulate to tell someone how pleased you are about something special that has happened to her

connect to join together

a b **c** d e f g h i j k l m n o p q r s t u v w x y z

conquer to beat in a battle or war

conscious (kon-shuss) awake and able to understand what is happening around you

consider to think carefully about something

considerable large
*a **considerable** amount of money*

considerate kind and thoughful in the way you behave towards other people

consonant any letter of the alphabet except a, e, i, o, u, and sometimes y

constable a policeman or policewoman

constellation a group of stars

construct to build

contain to have something inside

container anything that you can put other things into. Buckets, cups, bags, boxes, and jars are all containers.

contented happy with what you have

contents what is inside a container or a book

contest a competition

continent one of the seven very large areas of land in the world

continue to go on doing something

contract an agreement between two people or companies

contraction a shorter form of something
*The word 'can't' is a **contraction** of 'cannot'.*

contradict to say that someone is saying something that is not true

control to be in charge of something and be able to make it do what you want

convenient 1 easy to get at or use
2 the right time for something

convent a place where nuns live and work together

conversation talking and listening to another person

convict a criminal who is in prison

convince to make someone believe something

cook 1 to get food ready to eat by heating it
2 someone whose job is to cook

cookie a small, thin, cake

45

cool to lower the temperature

copper a shiny brown or red metal used for making pipes and coins

copy 1 to write down or draw what is already written down or drawn
She **copied** the poem in her best writing.
2 to do exactly the same as someone else

coral a kind of rock made in the sea from the bodies of tiny creatures. Coral can be pink, white, or black.

cord thin rope

core the part in the middle of something
an apple **core**

cork a piece of bark from a special kind of tree. It is put into the top of a bottle to close it.

corkscrew a tool for getting corks out of bottles

corn 1 a plant grown by farmers **2** the yellow kernels from this plant

corner the point where two edges or streets meet

cornet a musical instrument made of brass, that you blow

cornflakes a kind of food made from corn, eaten with milk at breakfast

cornet

coronation the time when someone is crowned as king or queen

corpse a dead body

correct without any mistakes

corridor a long, narrow way inside a big building or train. It has doors along it and people go down it to get from one room to another.

cosmonaut someone who travels in space

cost 1 to have a certain price
The bike **cost** a lot more before the sales
2 the price something is sold at

costume 1 clothes worn on the stage

2 clothes like ones worn long ago

cosy warm and comfortable

cottage a small house in the country

cotton a light cloth made from a plant that grows in hot countries
a cool **cotton** dress

couch a sofa

cougar a large wild cat, usual y brownish-yellow. It is sometimes called a mountain lion, but is smaller than an African lion.

cough (koff)
to make a sudden, loud noise to get rid of something in your throat. Smoke and bad colds make people cough.

could see **can**

council a group of people chosen to plan and decide what should be done in a place.
a city **Council**

count 1 to say the numbers in order
2 to use numbers to find out how many people or things there are in a place

counter 1 the long table where you are served in a store cafeteria, or bank
2 a small, round, flat piece of plastic used for playing some games

counter-clockwise in the opposite direction to the movement of a clock's hands

country 1 a land with its own people and laws. Canada, Australia, and China are all countries
2 the countryside

countryside land with farms and villages, away from towns

county one of the large areas that provinces like Ontario and New Brunswick are divided into

couple two
a **couple** of birds

coupon a kind of ticket that you can change for a free gift. Some coupons make you able to buy things for less money than usual.

courage a lack of fear
Champlain had great **courage** to sail to Canada. The people with him were **courageous** too.

course the direction something takes
a ship's **course**

court 1 a piece of ground marked out for a game like tennis
2 the place where a king or queen is living and the people who are with them
3 the place where people decide whether someone is guilty of breaking the law

cousin the child of your aunt or uncle

cover 1 to put one thing over or around another thing
2 something used for covering things

cow a female in the cattle family

coward someone who cannot face up to danger

cowboy a man who rides around looking after the cattle on a ranch

cowslip a yellow wild flower that grows in the spring

coyote a dog-like animal that looks like a small wolf

CPU *short for* Central Processing Unit. It is the part of the computer that controls all the computer's operation.

crab an animal with a shell, claws, and ten legs that lives in or near the sea

crack 1 to make the sudden, sharp noise a dry twig makes when you snap it
2 a line on the surface of something where it has been partly broken. Cracks can come in walls, ceilings, cups, and plates

cracker a thin biscuit eaten with butter or cheese

crackle to make the cracking sounds burning wood makes

cradle a baby's bed

craftsman someone who is very good at doing difficult work by hand

crafty clever at planning things so that you get your own way

crane 1 a machine on wheels for lifting very heavy things
2 a large bird with very long legs

cranky hard to please

crash 1 the loud noise made when something heavy is dropped and smashed
2 to hit something with a loud noise
*The dishes **crashed** to the floor.*

crate a container for carrying bottles or other things that break easily

crawl 1 to move on your hands and knees
2 to move slowly

crayon 1 a stick of coloured wax
2 a coloured pencil

crazy likely to do strange and silly things

creak to make a loud, rough, squeaking noise. New shoes, doors that need oiling, and old wooden stairs creak.

48

cream 1 the thick part on the top of milk
2 the colour of cream
3 something that looks like cream and is put on the skin
hand **cream**

crease to make a line in something by folding it

create to make something no one else has made or can make

creator someone who makes what no one else has made or can make

creature any animal

credit a promise to pay later
The farmer bought a tractor on **credit**

creek a small stream

creep 1 to move along, keeping close to the ground
2 to move quietly or secretly
We **crept** *away and nobody saw us.*

crepe paper (krape paper) thin, coloured paper that you can stretch

crept see **creep**

crescent a street shaped like a curved line

crew a group of people who work together on a boat or airplane

crib a baby's bed with bars

around it to stop the baby falling out

cricket 1 an insect that makes a shrill sound
2 a game played in a field by two teams with a ball, two bats, and two wickets

cried see **cry**

crime a bad deed that breaks the law

criminal someone who has done something bad that breaks the law

crimson a deep red colour

crinkle to make small lines in skin or paper by creasing it

crisp firm and fresh

criss-cross with lines that cross each other

croak to make the hoarse sound a frog makes

crocodile a reptile that lives in rivers in some hot countries. It has short legs, a long body, and sharp teeth

crocus a small white, yellow, or purple spring flower

crook 1 someone who cheats or robs people

2 a shepherd's stick with a curved top

crooked bent

crop 1 plants grown on a farm for food
2 to bite off the tops of plants. Sheep crop grass.

cross 1 to move across something
2 angry

crouch to lean forward and bend your knees so that you are almost touching the ground

crow a big, black bird

crowd a large number of people

crown a big ring of silver or gold worn on the head by a king or queen

cruel very unkind

cruise to sail without hurrying

crumb a tiny bit of bread or cake

crumble to break or fall into small pieces

crumple to make something very creased
crumpled *clothes*

crush to damage something by pressing it hard

crust the hard part around the outside of bread

crutch a wooden stick that a crippled person can lean on

when he is walking. It fits under the top of the arm
a pair of ***crutches***

cry 1 to let tears fall from your eyes
He was so upset that he ***cried.***
2 to shout

crystal a hard material like very bright glass

cub a young bear, lion, tiger, or wolf

Cub Scout a junior Boy Scout

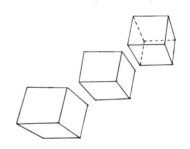

cube the shape of dice or sugar lumps. Cubes have six square sides that are all the same size.

cucumber a long, green vegetable eaten raw

cuddle to put your arms closely around a person or animal that you love

cuff the part joined to the end of a sleeve to fit around the wrist

culprit the person who is guilty

cunning crafty

cup a container for drinking or measuring

cupboard a piece of furniture or a space inside a wall. Cupboards have doors and usually some shelves.

cure to make well again

curiosity a wish to find out about things

curious 1 wanting to know about something
2 unusual
a **curious** smell

curl 1 a piece of hair twisted into rings
2 to curl up to sit or lie comfortably with the body bent around itself

currant a small, black, dried grape

current water, air, or electricity moving in one direction

curtain a piece of cloth pulled in front of a window or stage to cover it

curve a line that is bent smoothly like the letter C

cushion a cloth bag filled with soft material so that it is comfortable to sit on or rest against

custard a thick, sweet pudding

custom something that is usually done. It is a custom to give wedding presents

customer someone who buys at a store

cut 1 to use scissors or a knife to open, divide, or shape something
She's **cutting** out the picture.
I've **cut** up your meat for you.
2 an opening in the skin made by something sharp

cute pretty

cutlery knives, forks, and spoons

cycle to ride a bicycle

cylinder the shape of a soup can

cymbals a musical instrument that is two round pieces of metal that you bang together
a pair of **cymbals**

Dd

dad a word for father
*My **Dad** and Mom are upstairs.*

daffodil a yellow flower that grows from a bulb

dagger a short knife with two sharp edges

daily every day
*a **daily** paper*

dairy a place where milk is put in containers, and is made into butter and cheese

dam a wall built to hold water back. Some dams are built to stop floods.

damage to harm something

damp a little wet
***damp** grass*

dance to move about in time to music

dandelion a weed with a bright yellow flower

danger 1 something that may be harmful
2 the chance of something harmful happening
***danger** of fire*

dangerous likely to harm you
*It's **dangerous** to play in the road.*

dangle to hang loosely

dare 1 to be brave enough or foolish enough to do something
2 to ask someone to show how brave he is
*I **dare** you to climb that tree.*

daring very brave or very foolish

dark 1 without any light
*a **dark** house*
2 not light in colour
*a **dark** green coat*

darling someone who is loved very much

darn to sew over a hole in a garment to mend it

dart 1 to move very quickly and suddenly
2 a kind of short arrow that you throw

dash 1 to move very quickly
2 a mark like this -

data information about something

data processing the activity of a computer or similar device when it is working with information

date 1 the day, the month, and the year when something happens
2 a sweet, brown fruit that grows on a palm tree

daughter a girl or woman who is someone's child

dawdle to walk too slowly

dawn the time of the day when the sun rises

day 1 the twenty-four hours between midnight and the next midnight
2 the part of the day when it is light. (Also called daylight)

dazed not able to think properly
People are often dazed after an accident.

dazzle to be so bright that it hurts your eyes to look
*The sun was **dazzling**.*

dead without life

deaf not able to hear

deal 1 to give out
*I **dealt** the cards last time.*
2 to do a job that needs doing
*to **deal** with something*
3 a lot
*a great **deal***

dealt (delt)
see **deal**

dear 1 loved
2 Dear is always used to begin letters, for example Dear Uncle Ed...

3 costing a lot
*Cars are **dear***

death the end of life

debt something that you owe someone

decametre, decameter a measurement of ten metres

decay to go bad
*Too much sugar makes teeth **decay**.*

deceit a lie, something that is not true

deceive to make someone believe something that is not true

December the twelfth month of the year

decide to make up your mind about something

decimal 1 using tens
*the **decimal** system*
2 a way of writing fractions by putting numbers after a dot
$\frac{3}{10}$ *is* 0.3, $1\frac{1}{2}$ *is* 1.5

decimetre, decimeter ten centimetres, one-tenth of a metre

decision what you have decided

deck 1 a floor on a ship
2 a pack of cards

declare to say something important that you want everyone to know

decorate to make something look pretty

decrease to make smaller or fewer

deed something special that someone has done
a good **deed**

deep going a long way down from the top
deep water, a **deep** hole

deer a graceful animal that can move very quickly. Male deer have antlers growing out of their heads.
two **deer**

defeat to beat someone in a game or battle

defend to keep someone or something safe from attack

definite fixed or certain
a **definite** date for the holiday

definition an explanation of something
What is the **definition** of that big word?

defy to say or show that you will not obey

delay 1 to make someone or something late
2 to put off doing something until later

deliberate done on purpose
a **deliberate** mistake

delicate 1 soft and fine
delicate material
2 likely to get ill or damaged
a **delicate** child
delicate machinery

delicious tasting or smelling very pleasant

delight to please very much

deliver to bring things like milk or newspapers to someone's house

delivery delivering something

demand to ask for something that you think you ought to get

democracy a country that is ruled by its own citizens with a government that the citizens choose by voting
Canada is a **democracy**.

demolish to knock something down and break it up
a **demolished** house

demonstrate to show
She's **demonstrating** how it works.

demonstration a lot of people marching through the streets to show everyone what they think of something

54

den 1 the home of a wild animal **2** a room in a house for reading and other hobbies

dense thick
*a **dense** fog, a **dense** forest*

dent to make a hollow in something hard, by hitting it.
*Cars are often **dented** in accidents.*

dentist someone whose job is to look after teeth

deny to say that something is not true

depart to go away

depend to trust someone or something to give you the help you need
*The blind man **depends** on his guide dog.*

depress to make someone feel sad

depth how deep something is

descend (dis-send)
to go down

describe to say what something or someone is like

description words that tell you about someone or something

desert (*dez*-ert)
a very dry area of land where few plants can grow

deserted left by everyone
*a **deserted** house*

deserve to have done something that makes people think you should get a reward or a punishment
*He was so brave he **deserves** a medal.*

design to draw a plan or pattern for something

desire to want very much

desk a kind of table where you can write or study

despair to give up hope

desperate ready to do even dangerous or stupid things, because you have lost hope
*a **desperate** robber*

despise to dislike someone very much
*They **despised** him because he had cheated.*

dessert (diz-*ert*)
sweet food eaten after the main part of a meal

destination the place you are travelling to

destroy to damage something so badly that it cannot be used again

destroyer a small, fast ship for attacking other ships

destruction when something is destroyed

detail a tiny piece of information about something

detective someone who tries to find out who did a crime

determined with your mind firmly made up
determined to win

detest to hate

develop 1 to become bigger or better
2 to invent

device a tool or instrument that helps you do things

dew tiny drops of water that come during the night on things outside

diagonal a slanting line drawn from one corner of something to the opposite corner

diagram a kind of picture that explains something

dial a circle with numbers or letters round it. Clocks, watches, and telephones have dials.

dialect the special way people speak in certain parts of the country

diameter a straight line drawn across a circle, through the centre

diamond 1 a very hard jewel like clear glass
2 a shape with four sloping sides that are the same length. Some playing-cards have red diamonds printed on them.

diary a book where you can write down what happens every day

dictionary (*dik*-shun air-ee) a book where you can find out what a word means and how to spell it

did see **do**

die 1 to stop living
*The dog was **dying**.*
*The king has **died**.*
2 a small cube used in games. Each side is marked with a different number of spots from 1 to 6
*two **dice***

diesel (*rhymes with* weasel) an engine that burns oil to make power

diet special meals that some people must have to be healthy

difference how different one thing is from another thing

different not like someone or something else

difficult not easy
*a **difficult** question*

difficulty 1 something difficult
2 not easily
*He opened the window with **difficulty**.*

dig to move soil away to make a hole in the ground
*I **dug** a hole and planted the tree.*

digest to change the food in your stomach so that your body can use it

dignified looking serious and important

dim not bright

dime a coin worth ten cents

dimple a small hollow in the cheek or chin

dinosaur

dinghy (ding-ee) a small boat

dingy (din-jee) looking dirty
a **dingy** room

dining-room the room where people have their meals

dinner the main meal of the day

dinosaur a large animal that lived on the land millions of years ago

direct 1 to show someone the way
2 as straight and quick as it can be
the **direct** route

direction the way you go to get somewhere

dirt dust or mud

dirty marked with dirt or stains
a **dirty** face

disagree to think that someone else is wrong and you are right

disappear to go away and not be seen any more

disappoint to make someone sad by not doing what he hoped

disaster something very bad that happens suddenly

disciple a follower

discourage to try to stop someone doing something

discover to find out about something

discovery finding out about something

discuss to talk about something with people who have different ideas about it

57

a b c **d** e f g h i j k l m n o p q r s t u v w x y z

disease any illness

disgraceful so bad that it brings you shame
disgraceful work

disguise to make yourself look different so that people will not recognize you
*The thief **disguised** himself as a policeman.*

disgust hate for something nasty

dish a shallow bowl

dishonest not honest

disk a magnetic plate for storing information a computer can use. See **floppy disk**.

dislike the feeling you have for someone or something you do not like

dismal dark and sad

dismay to make someone lose hope and be afraid

dismiss to send someone away

display 1 to show
2 a show
*a dancing **display***

dissolve to mix something into a liquid so that it becomes part of the liquid. You can dissolve salt in water very easily

distance the amount of space between two places

distant far away

distinct 1 easy to see or hear
2 different

distress great sorrow, trouble, or worry

district part of a town, city, county, or country

disturb 1 to upset someone's peace or rest
2 to move something out of place

disturbance something that upsets someone's peace or rest

ditch a long, narrow hole. Ditches are dug to take away water from land.

dive to jump head first into water

divide 1 to share something among others
2 to split something into smaller parts
3 to find out how many times one number goes into another
*Six **divided** by two is three, 6÷2 = 3.*

dizzy feeling as if everything is spinning around you

do 1 to carry out an action
*She has to **do** her work now.*
*If she **doesn't** we cannot go.*
*What are you **doing**?*
***Don't** listen to them.*
2 to finish
*I **did** my work before I went out to play. He **didn't**.*

*Have you **done** your picture yet?*

dock a place where ships and boats are loaded, unloaded, or repaired

doctor someone whose job is to help sick people to get better

dodge to move quickly to get out of the way of something

doe a female deer or rabbit

does see **do**

dog a four-legged animal usually kept as a pet

doll a toy in the shape of a person

dollar an amount of money. Dollars are used in Canada, the United States of America, Australia, and some other countries.

dolphin an animal with warm blood that lives in the sea

dome a roof shaped like the top half of a ball

done see **do**

donkey an animal that looks like a small horse with long ears

doodle to scribble while you are thinking about something else

door a tall piece of wood that fills an opening in a wall. You can open a door to get into or out of a place.

double twice as much or as many

doubt (*rhymes with* out) the feeling you have when you are not sure about something

doubtful not sure

dough (*rhymes with* so) a mixture of flour and water. Dough is used for making bread and cakes.

doughnut a small cake that is fried and covered in sugar

dove a bird that looks like a small pigeon

down 1 to somewhere lower *Run **down** the hill.* **2** very soft feathers

doze to be nearly asleep

dozen a set of twelve

drab looking dull *drab clothes*

drag to pull something heavy along

59

dragon a monster with wings, that you read about in stories. Dragons breathe out fire and often guard treasure.

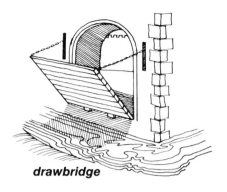

drawbridge

dragonfly a brightly coloured insect that lives near water

drain 1 a pipe for taking away water
2 to get rid of water by using pipes, ditches, or tiles

drake a male duck

drama a play or story

drank see **drink**

draught (*rhymes with* raft) cold air that blows into a room

draw 1 to do a picture with a pen, pencil, or crayon
*It was **drawn** in crayon.*
2 to end a game with the same score as the other side
*They **drew** 1-1 last Saturday.*

drawbridge a bridge over the water around a castle. It can be pulled up to stop people getting into the castle.

drawer a box without a lid, that slides into a piece of furniture

drawn see **draw**

dread great fear

dreadful very bad

dream to see and hear things while you are asleep
*Last night I **dreamt** about Christmas.*

drench to make someone very wet all over
*He was **drenched** by the rain.*

dress 1 to put clothes on
2 a piece of clothing that is like a skirt and blouse in one piece

dresser a piece of furniture with drawers for keeping clothes

drew see **draw**

drift 1 to be carried gently along by water or air
2 to pile up because of the wind
*Snow **drifted** onto the road.*

drill 1 a tool for making holes
2 to practise a lot

drink to swallow liquid
*Have you **drunk** your milk?*
*He was thirsty so he **drank** a lot.*

drip to let drops of liquid fall off

drive to make a machine or animal move
*He's never **driven** a bus before.*
*I **drove** the cows into the field last night.*
*He was **driving** too fast.*

driveway the short road that goes into someone's property

drizzle very light rain

droop to hang down weakly
*a **drooping** flower*

drop 1 a tiny amount of fluid
2 to let something fall

drove see drive

drowsy sleepy

drum a hollow musical instrument that you bang with a stick

drunk see **drink**

dry not damp or wet
dry land

dryer a machine for drying wet laundry

duck 1 a bird that lives near water. It has a wide, flat beak.

2 to bend down quickly to get out of the way

due 1 expected
*The train is **due** now.*
2 caused by
*The accident was **due** to the fog.*

duel a fight between two people using the same kind of weapon
*a **duel** with swords*

dug see **dig**

dull 1 not interesting
*a **dull** book*
2 not bright
*a **dull** colour*
3 not sharp
*a **dull** sound*

dumb not able to speak

dump 1 a place where rubbish is left
2 to leave something you want to get rid of
3 to put something down carelessly

dune buggy a light vehicle with very wide tires for driving in sand

dungeon (dunjun)
a prison underneath a building

during while something else is going on
*I fell asleep **during** the film.*

dusk the dim light at the end of the day, before it gets dark

dust 1 dry dirt that is like powder **2** to clear dust away from something

duty what you ought to do

duvet (doo-*vey*) a large, cloth bag filled with something soft like feathers and used instead of sheets and blankets on a bed

dwarf someone who is very small

dwindle to get smaller and smaller

dye to change the colour of something by putting it in a special liquid

dying see **die**

dynamite something very powerful that is used for blowing things up *a stick of* **dynamite**

each every single person or thing in a group *Each dog had a red collar.*

eager full of a strong wish to do something

eagle a large bird that eats mice, snakes, and small animals

eagle

ear 1 the part of the head used for hearing **2** the group of seeds on a stalk of grain

early 1 near the beginning *early in the day* **2** sooner than was expected *She came home* **early**.

earn to get money by working for it

earth 1 soil or dirt in which plants grow **2** (often capitalized) the planet on which we live

earthquake a time when the ground shakes

ease rest from pain and trouble

easel a stand for holding a blackboard or a picture while you work on it

east the direction of the rising sun

eastern from the east or in the east

easy 1 able to be done or

eel

understood without any trouble
an **easy** question
2 comfortable
an **easy** chair

eat to take food into the body
Has he **eaten** his dinner?
He **ate** it all five minutes ago.

ebb the movement of the sea
back from the land

eccentric likely to behave in a
strange way

echo a sound that is heard again
as it bounces back off
something solid. Echoes are
often heard in caves and
tunnels.

eclipse 1 a time when the
moon comes between the earth
and the sun so that the sun's
light cannot be seen
2 a time when the earth comes
between the sun and the moon
so that the moon's light cannot
be seen

edge the part along the end or
side of something

editor the person in charge of a
newspaper, magazine, or
comic. Editors decide which
stories and pictures should be
printed.

education the teaching and
learning of ideas and facts

eel a fish that looks like a snake

effect anything that happens
because of something else

effort hard work at something
you are trying to do

egg 1 a round object with a thin
shell, made by a hen and used
as food
2 one of the round objects that
baby birds, fish, insects, or
snakes live inside until they are
big enough to be born.

either one or the other of two
people or things
It's **either** right or wrong.

elastic a strip of material that
can stretch in length and then
go back to its former size

elbow the bony part in the
middle of the arm where it
bends

elder older than another person

election a time when people
can choose the men and
women who will be in charge of
their government
a General **Election**

electric worked by electricity

electricity power that moves along wires. Electricity is used for giving light and heat and for making machines work.

elephant a very big gray animal with tusks and a very long nose called a trunk, that it uses like an arm

elm a tall shade tree with curved branches

else besides
*Ask someone **else**.*

embarrass to make someone feel shy and upset

emblem a thing or a picture which is the special sign for a group, or a country, or an idea
*The beaver is an **emblem** for Canada.*

embrace to put your arms around someone

embroidery pretty sewing that decorates something

emerald a green jewel

emergency something very important that suddenly happens

emigrate to go and live in another country

empire a group of countries ruled over by one person

employ to pay someone to work for you

empty with nothing in it or on it

64

enamel 1 a kind of paint that gives a hard, shiny surface to things
2 the hard, shiny surface of your teeth

encourage to make someone brave and full of hope so that she will do something

encyclopedia a book or a set of books that tells you about all kinds of things

end 1 to be finished
*The movie will **end** in one hour.*
2 to finish
*The orchestra **ended** the concert.*

ending the end of something
*The **ending** of the movie was sad.*

endeavour, endeavor to try hard to do something

enemy 1 someone who wants to hurt you
2 the people fighting on the other side

energetic full of the strength for doing a lot of things

energy the strength to do things

engine a machine that is used to make things move

engineer someone who plans the building of roads, bridges, or machines

enjoy to like watching, listening to, or doing something

enormous very big

enough not less than is needed
enough money

enter 1 to come or go in
2 to take part in a race or a competition

entertain to make time pass very pleasantly for people

entertainment anything that entertains people. Shows, circuses, plays, and movies are entertainments.

enthusiasm a very great interest in something
an *enthusiasm* for football

enthusiastic so interested in something that you spend a lot of time on it and are always talking about it

entire whole
The *entire* class was ill.

entrance the way into a place

entry 1 a way into a place
2 going or coming into a place
3 a person, animal, or thing in a competition

envelope a paper cover for a letter

envious full of envy

environment the area around something or someone
Seals live in a wet
environment.

envy a feeling you get when you would like to have something that someone else has

equal the same as something else in amount, size, or value
equal shares

equator an imaginary line around the middle of the earth
Countries near the *equator* are very hot.

equipment the things you need to do something

eraser a thing used to rub out marks

erect standing or sitting straight up

erosion a wearing away because of the action of wind or water
The wind causes soil *erosion* in the prairie provinces.

errand a short journey to take a message or get something for someone

error a mistake

escalator a moving staircase

escape 1 to get free
2 to get away

especially more than anything else

estate 1 an area of land with a lot of houses on it
2 a large area of land that belongs to one person

estimate to guess the amount, size, or price

eve the day or night before a special day
*Christmas **Eve***

even 1 level or equal
*Our scores were **even**.*
2 that two will go into
*Six is an **even** number.*

evening the time at the end of the day before people go to bed

event something important that happens

eventually in the end

ever 1 at any time
*Have you **ever** read this?*
2 for ever, always

evergreen any tree that stays green all through the year

every each, all
***Every** week has seven days.*

everybody, everyone every person

everyday ordinary, not special
*Erin wears **everyday** clothes to play outside.*

everything all things

everywhere in all places

evil very wicked
*an **evil** deed*

ewe (you)
a female sheep

exact just right

exaggerate to make something sound bigger than it is

exam, examination an important test

examine to look at something very carefully

example 1 anything that shows how something works or what it is like
2 a person or thing that should be copied

excellent very good

except apart from
*Everyone got a prize **except** me.*

exchange to give something and get something in return

excite to interest someone so much that he has strong feelings such as love, fear, or anger
*an **exciting** film*

excitement an excited feeling

exclaim to make a sudden sound because you are surprised or excited

exclamation mark a mark like this! put after words to show strong feeling

excursion a trip out somewhere for the day or afternoon
*an **excursion** to the zoo*

excuse[1] (*ends in the sound* -s)

words that try to explain why you have done wrong so that you will not get into trouble

excuse[2] (*ends in the sound -z*) to forgive

execute 1 to do something or perform something
*Patty **executed** her half of the job very well.*
2 to put someone to death

exercise 1 work that makes your body healthy and strong
2 a piece of work that you do to make yourself better at something

exhausted tired out

exhibition a group of things put on show so that people can come to see them

exile someone who has to live away from his own country

exist 1 to be real, not imaginary
*Do fairies **exist**?*
2 to live

exit the way out of a place

expand to get bigger

expect to think something is very likely to happen

expedition a journey made in order to do something
*a climbing **expedition***

expensive with a high price
*an **expensive** car*

experience 1 what you learn from things that you have seen and done
2 something that has happened to you

experiment a test to find out whether an idea works

expert someone who does something very well or knows a lot about something

explain to make something clear to people so that they understand it

explanation something said or written to help people to understand

explode to make something blow up with a loud bang

explore to look carefully around a place for the first time

explosion a loud bang made by something blowing up

explosive anything used for making things blow up

express 1 a fast train
2 to put an idea or feeling into words

expression the look on someone's face

extension a part that has been added to make something bigger

extinguish to put out a fire

extra more than usual

extraordinary very unusual

extravagant always ready to spend a lot of money

extreme 1 very great
extreme cold
2 the furthest away
the *extreme* north

eye 1 the part of the head used for seeing
2 the small hole in a needle

eyebrow the curved line of hair above each eye

eyelash one of the short hairs that grow in a fringe around each eye

eyelid the piece of skin that moves to cover your eye

fable a story about animals that teaches people something

face 1 the front part of the head
2 a surface
A cube has six *faces*.
3 to have the front toward something
The church is *facing* the school.

fact anything that people know is true

factory a building where machines are used to make things

fade 1 to lose colour
faded curtains
2 to get paler or quieter so that it is harder to see or hear

fahrenheit (fair-en-hite) a way of measuring temperature that gives 32 degrees for freezing water and 212 degrees for boiling water

fail to try to do something but not be able to do it

failure someone or something that has failed

faint 1 weak
a *faint* cry
2 to feel so dizzy that everything goes blank and you fall down

fair 1 light in colour
fair hair
2 right or just
It's not *fair*.
3 a festival with competitions for the best animals, vegetables, and things made by hand.

fairly almost or quite
fairly good
I'm *fairly* sure.

fairy one of the tiny, magic people in stories

faith belief in someone or something

faithful always ready to help your friends and do what you have promised to do

fake something not valuable that is made to look valuable

fall 1 to come down suddenly
He's **fallen** off his bike.
I **fell** over yesterday.
2 the autumn

false 1 not real
false teeth
2 not true
a **false** friend

falter 1 to keep stopping and nearly falling over
2 to keep stopping while you are speaking

fame being famous
great **fame**

familiar well known to you
a **familiar** face

family parents and their children and grandchildren

famine a time when there is very little food

famous very well known

fan 1 a machine that spins and moves air around
2 someone who likes another person or a sport or a hobby very much

fancy 1 decorated
a **fancy** hat
2 fancy dress unusual

dressing-up clothes

fang a long, sharp tooth. Dogs, wolves, and snakes have fangs.

far a long way
far from home

fare the money people have to pay to travel on trains, buses, boats, or airplanes.

farewell goodbye

farm a piece of land where someone grows crops and keeps animals for food

farmer someone who keeps a farm

farther to a greater distance
I live **farther** away now.

fashion the way of dressing most people like to try and copy

fast 1 moving quickly
a **fast** car
2 quickly
Don't drive too **fast**.
3 to go without food

fasten 1 to close something so that it will not come open
2 to join something

fastener something used for fastening things

fat 1 with a very thick, round body
2 the white, greasy part of meat

fatal causing a person or animal

to die
a **fatal** *accident*

father a male parent

faucet a spout or tap which turns on or shuts off the flow of water into a sink or tub

fault something wrong that spoils a person or thing

favour, favor something kind you do for someone

favourite, favorite liked the most

fawn 1 a young deer
2 a light brown colour

fear 1 a feeling you get when you think something bad might happen to you
2 to be afraid of someone or something

feast a special meal for a lot of people

feat something brave or difficult that has been done

feather one of the many light, flat parts that cover a bird instead of hair or fur

fed see **feed**

feeble weak

feed 1 to give food to a person or animal
*I **fed** the cat last night.*
2 to eat
*The pigs are **feeding** now.*

feel 1 to touch something to find out what it is like
2 to know something inside yourself
*I **felt** sad yesterday.*

feeling something that you feel inside yourself, like anger or love

fell see **fall**

felt 1 see **feel**
2 a kind of cloth made from wool

female any person or animal that can become a mother

fence a kind of wall made of wood or posts and wire. Fences are put around gardens and fields.

fender a metal covering over a wheel
*The **fenders** on my bike keep water from splashing on me.*

fern a plant with leaves like feathers and no flowers

ferret a long, thin, brown animal much like a weasel

ferry a boat that takes people from one side of a piece of water to the other

abcdef**f** g h i j k l m n o p q r s t u v w x y z

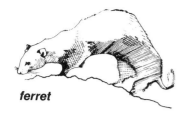

ferret

fertile able to make a lot of healthy plants
fertile soil

festival a time when people do special things to show that they are happy about something

fetch to go and get

fever an illness that makes people feel very hot and dizzy

few not many

fiddle 1 a violin
2 to play about with something

fiddlehead a slender curved fern that is good to eat when cooked

fidget to keep moving because you cannot keep still

field 1 a piece of ground with a fence around it and crops of grass growing on it
2 the place where games like football and soccer are played

field trip a visit by a class to some place to learn about it

fierce angry and frightening

fight to take part in struggle, battle, or war

We ***fought*** until it was dark.

figure 1 one of the signs for numbers, such as 1, 2, and 3
2 the shape of a body

file 1 a line of people one behind the other
2 a tool that is rubbed against things to make them smooth

fill to make someone or something full

film 1 a piece or roll of thin plastic put in a camera for taking photographs
2 moving photographs with sound that tell a story

filthy very dirty

fin one of the thin, flat parts that stand out from a fish's body and help it swim

final last
The ***final*** event is best.

finally at last

find to come across something, either by chance or because you have been looking for it
I've ***found*** my coat.

fine 1 very thin
fine material

71

2 dry and sunny
fine weather
3 very good
a *fine* picture
4 money someone has to pay as a punishment

finger one of the five separate parts at the end of the hand

fingernail a hard surface at the end of your fingers

fingerprint the mark left on the surface of something by the tip of a finger

finish to come to the end of something

fir a tall tree that has cones and leaves that look like green needles

fire the heat and bright light that come from burning things

fire escape a kind of steps or ladder used to get out of a building

fireplace an open place at the bottom of a chimney where a fire can be set

fireproof not able to catch fire and burn

firewood wood that is brought together for burning in a stove, furnace, or fireplace

fireworks paper tubes filled with a powder that will burn noisily and bang or send out coloured sparks and smoke

firm fixed so that it will not give away

first before all the others

fish 1 any animal with scales and fins that always lives and breathes under water
2 to try to catch fish

fisherman someone who catches fish

fist a hand with all the fingers pressed in toward the palm

fit 1 healthy
2 good enough
fit for a king
3 to be the right size and shape

fitness when your body is healthy and strong
Cecile believes in *fitness*.

fix 1 to join firmly to something
2 to mend

fizzy with a lot of tiny bubbles that keep bursting
fizzy drinks

flag a piece of coloured cloth

with a pattern on it, joined to a stick. Every country has its own flag.

flair a special ability for doing something
*Janet has a **flair** for public speaking.*

flake a very thin, light piece of something
*soap **flakes***

flame fire that is shaped like a pointed tongue

flannel a piece of soft cloth

flap 1 to move up and down like a bird's wings
2 a part that hangs down and is joined to the rest by one side. Envelopes have flaps.

flare to burn with a sudden, bright flame

flash to shine suddenly and brightly

flashlight a light with batteries that you can carry with you

flask a container that keeps hot drinks hot and cold drinks cold

flat not curved and with no bumps in it

flatten to make flat

flatter to praise someone too much

flavour, flavor how something tastes

flea a small insect without wings that sucks blood and jumps

flee to run away
*He saw the policeman and **fled**.*

flesh the part of the body that covers the bones

flew see fly

flight 1 a journey through the air
2 an escape
3 a set of stairs
*a **flight** of stairs*

flinch to move back slightly because you are afraid

fling to throw something as hard as you can
*I **flung** a stone and hit the giant.*

float 1 to be on the top of a liquid
2 to be carried along by liquid or air

flock a group of birds or sheep that feed together

flood a lot of water that spreads over land that is usually dry

floor the part of a building or room that people walk on

flop to fall or sit down suddenly

floppy disk a disk for storing computer information but which bends easily. See **disk.**

flour (*rhymes with* flower) a powder made from wheat and used for making bread, pastry, and cakes

flourish (flerish)
1 to grow well
2 to be happy and successful

flow to move along like a river

flower the part of a plant that is pretty and not coloured green

flown see **fly**

flu an illness that gives you a cold and makes you ache all over and feel very hot

fluff light, soft stuff that comes off wool, hair, or feathers

fluid any liquid or gas

fluke a piece of luck that makes you able to do something you thought you could not do

flung see **fling**

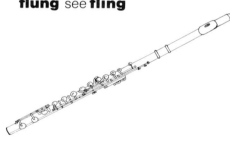

flute a long thin tube with holes in it. A flute is a musical wind instrument.

flutter 1 to keep moving the wings quickly, but not fly very far
2 to move a little, like a flag in a very light wind

fly 1 to move through the air with wings or in an airplane
*I **flew** from Hamilton to Saskatoon last week.*
*He's never **flown** before.*
2 a small insect with one pair of wings
*two **flies***

foal a young horse

foam 1 a lot of small bubbles on the top of a liquid
2 thick, soft rubber used for making sponges

fog damp air that looks like thick smoke and is difficult to see through

fold to lay one part of something on top of another part

folder a large cover made of cardboard for storing your work

foliage leaves

folk people

follow to go after

fond liking someone or something a lot
fond of fish

food anything that you eat to help you grow and be healthy

fool someone who is very silly

foolish silly

foot the part joined to the lower end of the leg
*two **feet***

football a game played by two teams who try to score goals by moving a ball past each other's goal line

footprint the mark left by a foot

footsteps the sound your feet make as you walk or run

for 1 in place of
*I will go to the store **for** you.*
2 in the amount of
*I have a bill **for** five dollars.*
3 the distance of
*Bill can see **for** a long way.*
4 toward
*They moved **for** the blue line.*
5 to find
*Everyone looked **for** the teacher.*
6 in exchange
*Tino traded his stick **for** a new puck.*
7 given to
*The juice is **for** you.*

forbid to say that someone must not do something
*She was **forbidden** to go out.*

force 1 to use your power to make a person, animal, or thing do something
2 a group of people with weapons
3 power

forecast saying what you think is going to happen before it happens
*a weather **forecast***

forehead the part of the face above the eyebrows

foreign belonging to another country
***foreign** coins*

forest a lot of trees growing together

forest fire a large fire in the forest

forest ranger a person who looks after a large section of forest

forgave see **forgive**

forge 1 to write or paint like someone else so that people will think he did it
2 to make a copy of something and pretend it is real
3 a place where metal is heated and shaped

forgery writing or a picture that is made to look as if someone else has done it

forget to fail to remember
*I've **forgotten** my lunch money.*
*I **forgot** the time and was late.*

forgive to stop being angry with someone
*Have you **forgiven** me?*
*I **forgave** him when he explained.*

forgot, forgotten see **forget**

fork a tool with three or four thin

pointed parts. People use small forks for picking up food and putting it into their mouths.

form 1 the shape something has
2 to make into
3 a special piece of paper where you write in information

former something that existed before now
*Matt's **former** house was in Victoria.*

fort a strong building for protection

fortress a big fort

fortunate lucky

fortune 1 a lot of money
2 luck

forward, forwards in the direction you are facing

fossil any part of a dead plant or animal that has been in the ground millions of years and become hard like rock

fought see **fight**

foul dirty and bad

found see **find**

foundation the solid part under the ground that a building is built on

fountain water that shoots up into the air

fowl any bird that is kept for its meat or eggs

fox a wild animal that looks like a dog and has a long, furry tail

fraction 1 a number that is not a whole number. ½, ¾, and ¼ are fractions
2 a very small part of something

fragile easily broken

fragment a small piece that has been broken off
***fragments** of rock*

frame 1 something that fits around the edge of a picture
2 a set of parts that fit together to give something its shape

frankfurter a wiener

fraud a trick or a person who tries to cheat someone

freak any person, animal, or thing with something very strange about it

freckle one of the small brown spots people sometimes get on their skin, when they have been in the sun

free 1 with nothing to stop you doing something or going somewhere
2 not costing anything
*a **free** gift*

freeze 1 to change into ice
*The pond **froze** last night.*
2 to be very cold
*Your hands will be **frozen**.*

frequent happening often
frequent rain

fresh 1 not old, tired, or used
fresh air, **fresh** bread,
a **fresh** start
2 not canned or preserved
fresh fruit

fret to keep worrying and getting upset about something

fridge *short for* refrigerator

friend someone you like who likes you. Friends like doing things together.

fright sudden fear

frighten to make someone afraid

frog a small animal with a smooth, wet skin. Frogs live near water and jump.

from out of
*He took a cookie **from** the jar.*

front the side that people usually see or come to first

frost ice that looks like powder and covers things when the weather is very cold

froth a lot of small bubbles on the top of a liquid

frown to have lines on your forehead because you are angry or worried

froze, frozen see **freeze**

fruit the seed of a plant and the

soft or juicy part around it

fry to cook in hot fat

frying-pan a large, shallow pan

fudge a kind of soft, very sweet toffee

fuel anything that is burned to make heat

full with no more room

fund money that will be used for something special

funeral the time when a dead person's body is buried

fungus a kind of plant that is not green and grows in damp places. Mushrooms and toadstools are both fungi.

funnel a tube with one very wide end to help you pour things into bottles

funny 1 amusing
*a very **funny** joke*
2 strange
*a **funny** smell*

fur the soft hair that covers some animals

furious very angry

furnace a very large machine like a stove, used to heat an entire building

furniture things such as beds and tables that you need inside a house and can move about

furrow the straight, narrow hollow made in the ground by a plough

furry covered in fur

further to a greater distance
*I swam **further** than you.*

furthermore in addition to

fuss to worry and bother too much about something that is not important

future the time that will come

fuzzy covered with short, soft hair

gadget a small, useful tool

gain to get something that you did not have before

galaxy a very large group of stars that belong together

gale a very strong wind

galleon a Spanish ship with sails, used long ago

gallery 1 a building or long room where paintings are shown
*an art **gallery***
2 the upstairs seats in a theatre or church

galley 1 a large boat used long ago that needed a lot of men to row it
2 the kitchen on a ship

gallop to move like a horse moving very quickly

gamble to try to win money when playing a game

game something that you play at that has rules. Football and hockey are games.

gander a male goose

gang a group of people who do things together

gangway 1 the plank or set of steps that people walk up to get on a boat

2 the path between rows of seats in a large building

gape 1 to have your mouth wide open with surprise
2 to be wide open

garage 1 the building where a car or bus is kept
2 a place that sells gasoline and repairs cars

garbage leftover things like food that are of no use

garden a piece of ground where flowers, fruit, or vegetables are grown

gargle to wash your throat by moving liquid around inside it

garment a piece of clothing

garter a band of elastic

gas 1 anything that is like air. Some gases have strong smells.
2 a gas that is burnt to make heat. see **gasoline**

gash a deep cut

gasoline a liquid fuel that makes machines, such as cars, run

gasp to breathe in noisily and quickly because you are surprised or ill

gate a kind of door in a wall or fence around a piece of land

gather 1 to bring together
2 to pick

gave see **give**

gay 1 cheerful
a gay time
2 brightly coloured
gay curtains

gaze to look at something for a long time

gear 1 the things needed for a job or sport
camping gear
2 part of a bicycle or car. Gears help to control the speed of the wheels so that it is easier to go up and down hills.

geese more than one goose

gem a valuable or beautiful stone

general 1 belonging to most people or things
2 an important officer in the army

generous always ready to give or share what you have

gentle quiet and kind

gentleman a polite name for a man

genuine real
Is that diamond genuine?

geography the study of different parts of the world

geranium a plant with red, pink, or white flowers that is often grown in a pot

gerbil (begins with the sound j-) a small, pale brown animal with long back legs and very soft fur. Gerbils dig holes in sand and are often kept as pets.

germ something that is alive but too small to see and helps to make people ill

get 1 to become
2 to take, buy, or be given something
I **got** a new bike yesterday.
I'm **getting** one for my birthday.

geyser a hot spring under the ground that shoots water and steam into the air

ghost the shape of a dead person that people think they have seen moving as if he were alive

giant one of the very big people in fairy stories

giddy 1 dizzy
2 silly
They sure are being **giddy** today.

gift a present

gigantic (jy-gantic) very big

giggle to keep laughing in a silly way because you cannot stop yourself

gill the part on each side of a fish that it breathes through

ginger a powder that gives a strong, hot taste

gingerbread a cake or thick biscuit that tastes of ginger

giraffe a very tall African animal with a very long neck

girl 1 a female child or teenager
2 a young woman

Girl Guide a member of a world-wide organization that encourages girls to be good citizens

give to let someone have something
Ken **gave** me an apple yesterday.
She was **given** first prize.
I'm **giving** you a second chance.

glacier a river of ice that moves very slowly down a mountain and along a plain

glad happy

glance to look at something quickly

a b c d e f **g** h i j k l m n o p q r s t u v w x y z

glare 1 to look angrily at someone
2 a very strong light

glass 1 something hard that you can see through. Glass is used for making windows.
2 a kind of cup that is made of glass and has no handle

glasses a pair of glass lenses held in front of the eye by a frame that fits over the nose and ears. People wear glasses to help them to see better.

gleam to shine with a soft light

glide to move very smoothly

glider a kind of airplane without an engine

glimmer a very weak light

glimpse to see something for only a few seconds

glisten to shine like something with drops of water on it

glitter to shine with a bright light that keeps coming and going
glittering *jewels*

globe a ball with the map of the whole world on it

gloomy 1 dark
*a **gloomy** room*
2 sad
*a **gloomy** face*

glory 1 great fame
2 great beauty

glossy smooth and shiny

glove a covering for the hand with separate parts for the thumb and each finger

glow to shine with the warm light a fire has

glue a thick liquid for sticking things together

glum not pleased or happy
*He looked **glum**.*

glutton someone who eats too much

gnarled (narled) twisted like the trunk of an old tree

gnat (nat) a thin fly that sucks blood

gnaw (naw) to keep biting something hard like a bone

gnome (nome) a kind of ugly fairy

go to move in any direction
*Her car **goes** very fast.*
*He's **gone** out to play.*
*They **went** on holidays yesterday.*
*When are you **going**?*

goal 1 the two posts the ball must go between to score a point in games like soccer
2 a point scored in hockey and other games

goalie the player who stands at the net in a game of hockey or soccer

gobble to eat very quickly and greedily

goblin a kind of bad, ugly fairy

goes see **go**

go-kart a kind of small, simple racing car

gold a valuable, shiny, yellow metal

golden coloured like gold

goldenrod a tall weed with yellow flowers

goldfinch

goldfinch a wild bird that is small, and black and yellow in colour

goldfish a small orange fish often kept as a pet

golf a game played by hitting small, white balls with sticks called clubs, over a large area of ground

gone see **go**

good something people like and praise
good work
2 kind and true
a *good* friend
3 well behaved
a *good* boy

goodbye the word you say when you are leaving someone

goods things that can be bought and sold

goose a water bird smaller than a swan, but larger than a duck, and with a longer neck. It may be tame and on farms, or wild and on the land around lakes or marshes.
see **Canada goose**
two geese

gooseberry a green berry that grows on a bush with thorns and can be cooked and eaten

gopher similar to a groundhog but smaller, lighter in colour, and quicker

gorgeous 1 very attractive
2 with bright colours

gorilla an African animal like a very large monkey with long arms and no tail

gosling a young goose

gossip 1 to talk a lot in a friendly way to someone
2 to talk a lot about other people

got see **get**

govern to be in charge of a place and decide what should happen there

government the group of people who are in charge of what happens in a country

Governor-General in Canada, the person who takes the place of the Queen at special times

grab to take hold of something suddenly

grace 1 beauty in the way someone moves or stands
2 a short prayer before or after a meal

grade 1 a class in school
Sarah is in **grade** *two.*
2 a mark or score
Timmy got a high **grade** *on his story.*
3 a short hill
You must climb that **grade** *to get there.*

gradual happening a little at a time
a **gradual** *change*

grain seed that grows in plants like corn and is used for making food

gram a tiny measure
one thousand **grams** *= one kilogram*

grand large, important, or wonderful

grandchild the child of a son or daughter. Granddaughters and grandsons are grandchildren.

grandfather the father of a father or mother

grandmother the mother of a father or mother

granite a very hard rock

grant to agree to give someone what he has asked for

grape a small, soft green or purple fruit that grows in bunches

grapefruit a fruit that looks like a big orange, but is yellow

graph (graf)
a diagram that helps you to see how numbers or amounts of things are different from each other

graphics pictures, charts, or other shapes drawn by a computer or by a designer

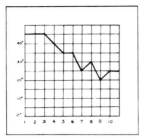

graph

grasp to get hold of something and hold it tightly

grass a green plant with flat, narrow leaves that can be eaten by cattle and other animals

grasshopper an insect that can jump a long way

grate 1 a container made of metal bars. Grates hold the coal or wood in a fire.
2 to rub something against a rough surface so that it falls into tiny pieces
3 to make the kind of noise the nail on your finger makes if you rub it against a blackboard.

grateful full of a wish to thank someone for what he has done

grave 1 the hole in which a dead person is buried
2 very serious

gravel a mixture of sand and tiny stones

gravity the force that pulls everything towards the earth. If there was no gravity everyone would fall off the earth and float out into space.

gravy a hot brown liquid that is poured over meat before it is eaten

gray a colour

graze 1 to hurt the skin by rubbing hard against something
2 to eat grass as it grows. Cows and sheep graze in fields.

grease thick, slippery stuff like oil

great 1 large
*a **great** amount of money*
2 important
*a **great** man*
3 very good
*a **great** idea*

greed a wish for much more food and money than you really need

green a colour

greenhouse a glass building for growing plants in

greet to welcome someone or say hello

grew see **grow**

grey see **gray**

grief a very sad feeling

grill to cook food on metal bars put under or over heat
*a **grilled** hamburger*

grim 1 not looking kind, friendly, or pleased
a **grim** face
2 not pleasant
grim weather

grin a smile that shows the teeth

grind to crush into tiny bits
The wheat was **ground** into flour.

grip to hold tightly

grit tiny bits of stone or sand

groan to make a low sound because you are in pain or trouble

grocer someone who keeps a store that sells food, drink, and things like soap and matches

groom 1 someone whose job is to look after horses
2 to make an animal look smart by cleaning and brushing it

groove a long, narrow hollow. Records have grooves in them.

grope to try to find something by feeling for it when you cannot see

ground 1 the earth
2 a piece of land
3 see **grind**

groundhog a small, brown furry animal with short legs

group a number of people,

groundhog

animals, or things that belong together in some way

grow 1 to become bigger
You've **grown** very quickly.
2 to plant something in the ground and look after it
We **grew** huge leeks last year.

growl to make a deep, angry sound. Angry dogs growl.

grown see **grow**

grove a small group of trees

grub a tiny creature that will become an insect

grudge a bad feeling you have against someone, because you think he has harmed you

gruel thin cooked cereal or porridge

gruff with a deep, rough voice

grumble to keep on saying that you are not pleased about something
Stop **grumbling**!

grunt to make the sound a pig makes

guard to keep someone or something safe from other people

guardian someone who is put in charge of a child whose parents cannot look after him

guess to say what you think the answer is when you do not really know

guest someone who is invited

guide 1 someone or something that shows people which way to go
2 a dog trained to help a blind person
guide dog

guilt 1 the fact that someone has done something wrong
2 a feeling you have when you know you have done something wrong

guilty full of guilt

guinea pig a small animal that has no tail and is kept as a pet

guitar a musical instrument with strings across it that you play with your fingers

gulf water that fills a very large bend in the land

gulp to swallow very quickly
I *gulped* down my tea and rushed out.

gum 1 the hard pink part of the mouth that holds the teeth
2 a candy that you chew
3 glue

gun a weapon that shoots bullets or pellets

gurgle to make the noise water makes as it goes down the hole in a bath

gush to move like water rushing out of a tap

gust a sudden rush of wind or air

gutter a long, narrow hollow at the side of a street or along the edge of a roof. Gutters take away rain water

gym a class for learning sports or for fitness

gymnasium a large room for holding games or for exercise

habit anything that you do without thinking, because you have done it so often

had see **have**

haddock an ocean fish that can be eaten

haggard looking ill and very tired
*a **haggard** face*

hail small pieces of ice that fall from the sky like rain

hair a soft covering that grows on the heads and bodies of people and animals

haircut a trim of your hair to make it shorter and neater

hairdresser someone whose job is to cut people's hair, wash it, or arrange it in a special way

half one of the two equal parts something can be divided into. It can also be written as ½.
*Two **halves** make a whole.*

hall 1 the part inside a house that leads from one room to another
2 a very big room
*a school **hall***
3 a large, important building or house
*the Town **Hall***

Halloween the last day of October. Many people wear costumes on this day and think that magic things happen.

halt to stop

halter 1 a rope or strap put around an animal's head or neck so that it can be controlled
2 a piece of clothing worn on the top half of the body

halve to divide into two equal parts

halves more than one half

ham one kind of meat from a pig

hamburger 1 beef that has been ground into small bits
2 ground beef cooked in a round shape and served on a bun

hammer a heavy tool used for hitting nails

hammock a bed that is a piece of cloth hung from something by cords joined to each corner

hamper 1 a big basket with a lid
*a picnic **hamper***
2 to make it difficult for someone to do something

hamster a small brown animal that has smooth fur and is kept as a pet

hand the part joined to the lower end of the arm

handbag a small bag or purse used to carry items

handcuffs a pair of metal rings used for locking someone's wrists together

handicap anything that makes it more difficult for you to do something

handkerchief a square of cloth carried in a pocket or handbag

handle 1 a part put on something so that you can get hold of it
2 to touch, feel, hold, or use something with your hands

handsome attractive

hang to fix the top part of something to a hook or nail
I **hung** up my coat.

hangar a shed for storing an airplane

hanger something used for hanging up clothes

happen 1 to take place
This must not **happen** again.
2 to do something by chance
I just **happened** to see it.

happiness the feeling you have when you are very pleased and enjoying yourself

happily 1 with joy
MaryPat sang **happily.**
2 luckily
The rope broke but **happily** no one was hurt.

happy full of happiness

harbour, harbor a place where boats can stay safely in the water when they are not out at sea

hard 1 not soft
hard ground
2 difficult
hard questions
3 severe
a **hard** punishment

hardly only just
hardly able to walk

hare an animal like a big rabbit that can move very quickly

harm to hurt or spoil someone or something
Poison can be **harmful** if you swallow it.

harmonica a small wind instrument with holes in it. It is sometimes called a mouthorgan.

harness the set of straps and buckles put over a horse so that it can pull things

harp a musical instrument. It has a large frame with strings stretched across it that are played with the fingers.

harsh not kind or gentle
a **harsh** voice

harvest the time when farmers gather in the fruit, corn, or vegetables they have grown

has see **have**

haste hurry

hat a cover for the head

hatch to break out of an egg. Baby birds, insects, fish, and snakes hatch.

hatchet a light tool like an axe for chopping

hate to have a very strong feeling against someone or something you do not like

haughty very proud of yourself

haul to pull or carry something from one place to another

haunted often visited by ghosts
a **haunted** house

have 1 to own
She **has** a new car.
We **haven't** got a car.
2 to contain
The box **had** candy in it.
It **hasn't** any in it now.
3 to enjoy or suffer
We're **having** a good time
He's **had** an accident.

hawk a bird that hunts smaller animals like mice and snakes

hay dry grass used to feed animals

haze damp or hot air that it is difficult to see through

head 1 the part of a person or animal that contains the brain and face
2 the person in charge
3 the top or very important part of something
a **head** of cabbage or grain

headache a pain in the head that goes on hurting

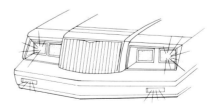

headlight a light at the front of a car or other vehicle

89

heal 1 to make well again
2 to become well again
The cut **healed** *quickly.*

health 1 the state of someone's body and mind
2 good health

healthy 1 not ill or injured in any way
2 good for people's health
healthy *air*

heap an untidy pile

hear to take in sounds through the ears
I **heard** *you shout so I came.*

heart 1 the part of the body that makes the blood go around
2 the curved shape of a heart. Red hearts are printed on some playing cards.

heat 1 the hot feeling that comes from the sun or a fire
2 to make hot

heave to lift or pull something heavy

heaven 1 the place where God is thought to be
2 a very happy place

heavy weighing a lot. It is difficult to lift and carry heavy things.

hectare a square measure of land that is one hundred metres long on all four sides

hedge a kind of wall made by bushes growing close together

heel the back part of the foot

height how high something is
a **high** *place*

heir (air) someone who will be given money, property, or a title when the owner dies

heiress a girl or woman who will be given money, property, or a title when the owner dies

helicopter a kind of small airplane that can rise straight up into the air. It has large blades that spin around on its roof.

helm the handle or wheel that is used to steer a ship.

helmet a strong covering that protects the head
a crash **helmet**

help to do something useful for someone else

helpless not able to look after yourself. Babies are completely helpless.

hem the edge of a piece of cloth, that is folded under and sewn down

hen a female bird, usually a chicken

herb a plant used in cooking to give the food a better flavour

herd a number of cattle that feed together

here in or to this place
*Come **here**!*

hermit someone who lives alone and keeps away from everyone else

hero a boy or man who has done something very brave

heroine a girl or woman who has done something very brave

herring a sea fish that can be eaten

herself 1 she and no one else
2 by herself on her own

hesitate to wait a little before you do or say something, because you are not sure about it

hibernate to sleep for a long time during the cold weather. Bats, turtles, and bears hibernate.

hiccup to make a sudden, sharp sound in the throat. People hiccup when they have eaten or drunk very quickly or laughed a lot.

hide 1 to get into a place where you cannot be seen
*I'm **hiding** over here.*
*I **hid** behind the tree last time.*
2 to put into a secret place
*The gold was **hidden** in a cave.*

hiding-place a place where someone or something is hidden

high 1 going a long way up
*a **high** mountain*
2 a long way up
*It flew **high** into the air.*

highway a public road, usually an important one

hijack to take control of a vehicle while it is flying and make it go where you want it to go

hill ground that is higher than the ground around it

himself 1 he and no one else
2 by himself on his own

hind the back or rear
*Our cat has a sore **hind** leg.*

hinder to get in someone's way so that it is difficult for her to do something

hinge a metal fastener that joins a door to a wall and lets the door swing backward and forward

hint 1 a useful idea
2 to give someone information without telling him exactly what you mean

hip the bony part of the body that sticks out at the side between the waist and thigh

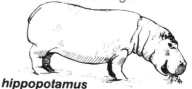

hippopotamus

hippopotamus a very large, heavy, African animal that lives near water. It has very thick skin.

hire 1 to give a job to
*Mom **hired** a new worker.*
2 to rent
*We will **hire** a truck to move our furniture.*

hiss to make the long sss sound that snakes make

history finding out about things that happened in the past

hit to strike with force
*Michael **hit** the nail with a hammer.*

hitch to tie or fasten
*The farmer **hitched** a wagon to the tractor.*

hitchhike to travel by asking for rides. A hitchhiker holds out his thumb to ask.

hive a kind of box for keeping bees in

hoard a secret store of money or other things

hoarse sounding rough and deep. People with sore throats have hoarse voices

hobby something interesting that people like doing in their spare time

hockey a game played on ice, or a field, between two teams who have curved sticks to move a puck or ball. Players wear skates for ice hockey.

hoe a tool for getting rid of weeds

hog 1 a large pig
2 a greedy or selfish person

hold 1 to have something in your hands
*I **held** up the picture I had done.*
2 the place inside a ship where things are kept

holdup 1 a robbery
2 a slowing down or stopping of something

hole a gap or opening made in something

holiday time off from school or work

hollow 1 with an empty space inside
*a **hollow** Easter egg*
2 a kind of hole

holly a tree that has shiny, prickly leaves and red berries in the winter

holster a case for putting a gun in. Holsters are worn on straps or belts.

holy something that is special in a religion

home the place where you live

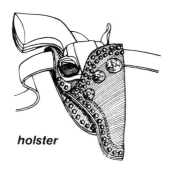

holster

home run a hit in baseball that allows the batter to go all the way around the bases

homesick the feeling you get when you want to be at home while you are somewhere else

homework schoolwork you have to do at home

honest not stealing, cheating, or telling lies
an **honest** *person*

honey sweet, sticky food made by bees

honour, honor great respect

hood a covering of soft material for the head and neck

hoof the hard part around a horse's foot

hook a piece of bent metal for hanging things on or catching hold of something

hoop a big wooden or metal ring used in games

hoot to make the sound made by an owl or the horn in a car

hop a small jump

hope to want something that you think is likely to happen

hopeless 1 without hope
2 very bad at doing something

hopscotch a game where you hop and throw or kick a stone into squares drawn on the ground

horizon the line where the sky and the land or sea seem to meet

horizontal 1 flat and level
2 a straight line across something
a **horizontal** *line*

horn 1 a kind of pointed bone that grows on the heads of some animals. Bulls and rams have horns.
2 a brass musical instrument that you blow

horrible 1 nasty
a **horrible** *sight*
2 frightening
a **horrible** *film*

horrid nasty
a **horrid** *dream*

horror very great fear

horse an animal with hooves that is used for riding and pulling

horseshoe a flat piece of metal fixed underneath a horse's hoof and shaped like this Ω

hose a long plastic or rubber tube that water can go through

hospital a place where people who are ill or hurt are looked after

hotel a building where people pay to have meals and stay for the night

hound a dog used for hunting

hour sixty minutes

house a building where people live together

household all the people who live together in the same house

hover to stay in one place in the air

hovercraft a machine that is like both an airplane and a boat. It travels quickly just above the surface of land or water.

how in what way
How did you cook the eggs?

howl to give a long, loud cry

hub the part at the centre of a wheel, where the spokes meet

huddle to keep close to others in a group because you are cold or frightened

huge very big

hull the main part of a boat or ship

hum 1 to sing a tune with your lips closed
2 to make the sound a bee makes

human any man, woman, or child

humble not proud
a *humble* person

hummingbird a very small bird with a long beak. Its wings make a humming sound when it flies

humorous amusing

hung see **hang**

hunger the need for food

hungry feeling hungry

hunt 1 to go after a wild animal because you want to kill it
2 to look carefully for something

hurl to throw something as far as you can

hurrah, hurray a word that

you shout when you are very
glad about something

hurricane a storm with a very
strong wind

hurry 1 to move quickly
2 to try to do something quickly
because there is not enough
time

hurt to make a person or animal
feel pain
*I **hurt** my knee when I fell down.*

hurtle to move very quickly

husband a man married to
someone

hustle 1 to hurry
2 to push someone roughly

hutch a kind of house for
keeping a rabbit

hyacinth a flower that grows
from a bulb and has a very
sweet smell

hymn a song of praise

hyphen a mark like this - used
in writing to join words or parts
of words together

I a word that you use instead of
your own name
I am very tired now.

ice water that has frozen hard

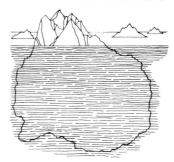

iceberg a large piece of ice
floating in the sea

ice cream a sweet frozen food
that tastes of cream

icicle a thin, pointed piece of ice
hanging down

icing a sweet, sticky mixture
spread over the tops of cakes to
decorate them

I'd a short form of I had, I would
*I'd a dog of my own once. (I
had)*
*I'd move that bicycle now if I
were you! (I would)*

idea 1 something you have
thought of yourself
2 a plan

ideal just what you want

identical exactly the same
identical twins

idle doing nothing
idle hands

idol something people worship
and treat as if it were God

if 1 in case, in the event that
If Sean is late, start anyway.
2 whether
*Stephen does not know **if** he plays his game tomorrow.*

igloo a round house made of blocks of hard snow

ignition the point at which something starts

ignorant knowing nothing or only a little

ignore to take no notice of someone

ill not well

illness something that makes people ill. Measles, chickenpox, and colds are illnesses.

illumination the lighting in a place like a building or a park

illustrate to make clear by examples or pictures
*Hope **illustrated** her talk about motorcycles with a film.*

illustration a picture in a book

image 1 a picture or other likeness of a person or thing

*See your **image** in the water.*
2 the way someone thinks he looks to others

imaginary not real

imagination the ability to make pictures in your mind of things and people you cannot see

imagine to make a picture in your mind of someone or something you cannot see

imitate to copy a person or animal

imitation a copy that is not as valuable as the real thing
***imitation** cream*

immediately straight away

immense very big

impatient anxious, unable to wait

implore to beg someone to do something for you

important 1 powerful and worth respect
*a very **important** person*
2 worth looking at or thinking about seriously
*an **important** notice*

impossible not possible

impress to make people think you are very good at something

impression an idea you have that may be wrong

impressive so wonderful that

you will always remember it

imprison to put someone in prison

improve 1 to become better
2 to make something better

incense something that gives you a sweet smell when it is burned

in 1 into
*Please come **in** the room.*
2 at home, indoors
*Trevor stayed **in** because of the rain.*
3 inside
*The pig is **in** the pen.*

include to make something part of a group of other things

income the money a person earns

income tax the money that people must give to the government out of the income they earn

incorrect not correct

increase 1 to make bigger
2 to become bigger

indeed really
*very wet **indeed***

independent not needing the help or control of others

index a list at the back of a book. It tells you what things are in the book and where to find them.

Indian 1 a native person of North or South America
2 a person who is a citizen of India

indignant angry because something unfair has been done or said

indoors inside a building

industry 1 hard work
2 work done in factories

infant a young child

infectious likely to spread to others
*an **infectious** illness*

inform to tell someone something

information words that tell people about something

infuriate to make very angry

ingenious clever at thinking of new ways of doing or making things

inhabit to live in a place

initial (in-ish-ul)
the first letter of a name
*William Brown's **initials** are W.B.*

injection a prick in the skin made by a hollow needle filled with medicine so that the medicine goes into the body

injure to harm

injury harm done to part of the body

ink a coloured liquid used for writing with a pen

inland in a part of the country that is not near the sea

inn a kind of small hotel

inning the time it takes for the two teams to bat in a baseball game

innocent not guilty

inquiry 1 a question
2 a search to find out all about something

inquisitive full of a wish to know about something

insect a tiny creature with six legs. Flies, ants, butterflies, and bees are all insects.

inside 1 in something
2 the part nearest the middle

insist to be very firm in saying or doing something
He **insists** on staying up late.

insolent very rude
insolent behaviour

inspect to look carefully at people or things

inspector 1 someone whose job is to check that things are done properly
2 an important policeman

instalment 1 an amount of money people pay each week or every month in order to buy something

2 a part of a story that is told in parts

instantly at once

instead in place of something else

instinct something that makes animals do things
Spiders spin webs by **instinct**.

instruction words that tell people what to do

instructor a kind of teacher

instrument 1 a tool or something else used for doing a job
2 something used for making musical sounds

insult to hurt someone's feelings by being rude

intelligent able to learn and understand things easily

intend to mean to do something

intense very great
intense heat

intercom a loudspeaker system for talking from one room to another

interest to make someone want to find out more, look, or listen

interface when two or more parts of a computer work together

interfere 1 to get in the way
2 to take part in something that

has nothing to do with you

international belonging to more than one country
*an **international** competition*

interrupt to stop someone from carrying on with what he is saying or doing

interview to ask someone questions to find out what she thinks about something or what she is like

introduce to make someone known to other people

invade to go into another country to fight against the people there

invalid someone who is weak because he is ill or injured

invent to be the first person to think of a plan for a new machine or a better way of doing something

investigate to try to find out as much as you can about something

invisible not able to be seen
invisible ink

invitation words that ask you politely to come
*a party **invitation***

invite to ask someone politely to come or do something

iron 1 a strong, heavy metal
2 a flat piece of metal with a handle. It is heated and used for making clothes smooth and flat.

irritable easily annoyed

irritate to keep annoying someone

island, isle a piece of land with water all around it

it a word you use in place of the name of a thing or animal just mentioned
*The moose jumped but **it** could not get over the fence.*

it's a short form for it is
It's very warm in the arena.

its a way of writing or saying its own
*The fox hurt **its** paw.*

italic 1 a kind of writing
2 *a kind of printing like this*

itch a feeling in your skin that makes you want to scratch yourself

item any one thing in a list or group of things

itself 1 it and nothing else
2 by itself on its own

ivory 1 something that comes from the tusks of elephants. It is pale cream-coloured, hard, and very valuable.
2 the pale cream colour of ivory

ivy a climbing plant with shiny dark green leaves

Jj

jab to push roughly at something with your finger, fist, or the end of a stick

jacket a kind of short coat

jack-o-lantern a hollow pumpkin with a face cut into it, and a candle inside

jagged with sharp parts along the edge

jail a building where prisoners are kept

jam 1 fruit boiled with sugar until it is thick
raspberry **jam**
2 a lot of people or cars crowded together so that it is difficult to move
a traffic **jam**
3 to become fixed and difficult to move
The door has **jammed** *and I can't open it.*

jar a container like the glass ones used for jam

jaw the lower part of the face

jaywalk to cross the street at the wrong time or place

jealous unhappy because someone else seems to have more or be doing better than you

jeans strong cotton trousers

jeep a very strong small car

jeer to make fun of someone because you think you are better than he is

jelly a sweet, shiny, slippery food that looks solid, but melts in your mouth
orange **jelly**

jerk to move suddenly or clumsily

jet 1 a liquid or gas coming very quickly out of a small opening
2 an airplane with an engine that is driven by jets of hot gas

jewel a valuable and beautiful stone

jewellery necklaces, bracelets, rings, and brooches

jigsaw puzzle a set of small pieces of cardboard or wood that fit together to make a picture

jingle to make the sound tiny bells make

job work that you do

jockey someone who rides horses in races

jog to run slowly

join 1 to put together to make one thing
2 to become a member of a group

joint the place where two parts fit together. The ankle is the joint between the foot and the leg.

joke something said or done to make people laugh

jolly happy and gay

jolt to shake suddenly

journey the travelling people do to get from one place to another place

joy great happiness

joystick one of the controls on a video game. It is grasped by hand and bent and turned while playing the game. Also called **paddle.**

judge 1 to decide whether something is good or bad, right or wrong, fair or unfair
2 someone who judges

juggler someone who entertains people by doing

difficult throwing, catching, and balancing tricks

juice the liquid in fruit and vegetables

jumble a lot of different things all mixed up

jump to move up suddenly from the ground into the air

junction a place where roads or railway lines meet

jungle a forest in a very hot, damp country

junior younger

junk things that people do not want any more

just 1 fair
a **just** king
2 exactly
It's **just** what I wanted.
3 only
Just one more cookie please.

K a computer language short form for 1024 bits. It tells you how much information a computer can store away.

kaleidoscope a thick tube you look through to see coloured patterns. The pattern changes

101

when you turn the end of the tube.

kangaroo an Australian animal that jumps. Female kangaroos have pouches in which they carry their babies.

keen very interested in something

keep 1 to have something as your own and not get rid of it
He **kept** the money he found.
2 to make something stay as it is
3 to look after something

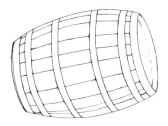

keg a small barrel

kennel 1 a small house for keeping a dog

2 a row of pens where dogs are kept by someone who sells them

kept see **keep**

kernel 1 the part in the middle of a nut
2 one of the pieces in an ear of corn or head of grain

kettle a metal container in which water is boiled. It has a lid, handle, and spout.

key 1 a piece of metal shaped so that it fits into a lock
2 a small lever pressed with the finger. Pianos and typewriters have keys.

kick to hit something with your foot.

kid 1 a word often used instead of "child"
2 a young goat

kidnap to take someone away and keep as a prisoner until you get what you want

kill to make someone or something die

kilogram a measure of mass
a **kilogram** of apples

kilometre, kilometer a measure for length
one **kilometre** = one thousand metres

kilt a kind of pleated skirt

kind 1 ready to help and love other people

2 a sort
*a special **kind** of paint*

kindling small pieces of wood used to start a fire

king a man who has been crowned as ruler of a country

kingdom a land that is ruled by a king or queen

kingfisher a brightly coloured bird that lives near water and catches fish

kiss to touch someone with your lips because you are fond of him or her

kitchen the room where food is cooked

kite a light frame covered in cloth or paper and flown in the wind

kitten a very young cat

knee the bony part in the middle of the leg where it bends

kneel to get down on your knees
*They **knelt** down and prayed.*

knew see **know**

knife a tool with a long, sharp edge for cutting things
*two **knives***

knight 1 a man who has been given the title, Sir
*Sir Francis Drake was a **knight.***
2 a man in armour who rode into battle on a horse

knit to use wool and a pair of long needles to make clothes

knives more than one knife

knob the round handle on a door or drawer

knock 1 to tap on a door
2 to bump something

knot the twisted part where pieces of string, rope, cotton, or ribbon have been tied together

know 1 to have something in your mind that you have found out
*I **knew** all about it yesterday.*
2 to have met someone before
*I haven't **known** her long.*

knowledge things that are known and understood

known see **know**

knuckle one of the places where the fingers bend

koala bear

koala bear a furry Australian animal that looks like a small bear

label a piece of cardboard or sticky paper put on something to show what it is, whose it is, or where it is going

laboratory a room or building where scientific work is done

labour, labor work that people do

lace 1 thin, pretty material with a pattern of holes in it. Lace is often used to decorate things. **2** a piece of thin cord used to tie up a shoe

lack to be without something

lad a boy or young man

ladder two long bars with short bars between them so that you can climb up or down

ladle a big, deep spoon used for serving soup

lady a polite name for a woman

ladybug a red or yellow insect with black spots on it

lag to be behind because you are moving too slowly
*He's **lagging** behind again.*

laid see **lay**

lain see **lie**

lair a wild animal's home

lake a large area of water with land all around it

lamb a young sheep

lame not able to walk properly

lamp something that gives light where you want it

lance a long spear like the ones used by knights long ago

land 1 all the dry parts of the earth's surface

2 a country
3 to arrive by boat or airplane

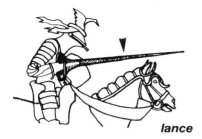

lance

landing the flat place at the top of the stairs in a building

landlady a woman who lets other people live in her house in return for money

landlord a man who lets other people live in his house in return for money

lane 1 a narrow road
2 a driveway into a farm
3 one of the sections on a highway or road where vehicles may drive

language words spoken or written by people
foreign languages

lantern a container for a light. It is made of metal and glass or something else that the light can shine through.

lap 1 the part from the waist to the knees of a person sitting down
2 once around a race track
3 to drink like a dog using your tongue

lard white fat from pigs, used in cooking

large big

lark 1 a small, bird that sings
2 a happy or silly adventure

lash 1 to tie tightly to something
2 to hit hard, usually with a whip

lasso (las-soo)
a long rope with a loop at the end, tied so that the loop can get bigger or smaller. Cowboys use lassos for catching cattle.

last 1 after all the others
2 to go on for some time

latch a fastener on a gate or door

late 1 after the expected time
2 near the end of a day, month, or year
3 no longer alive
the late Mrs. Smith

later after a time

lather soap bubbles on the top of water

laugh to make sounds that show that you are happy or think something is very funny

laughter the sound of laughing

launch 1 a large boat with an engine
2 to push a boat into the water
3 to send a space ship from earth into space

laundromat a place with

washing-machines that people can pay to use

laundry 1 clothes that need to be washed
2 a place where people send dirty clothes and sheets to be washed

lavender a pale purple colour

law a rule or set of rules that everyone in a country must obey

lawn the part of a garden that is covered with short grass

lawyer a person who explains laws

lay 1 to put something down
Lay the book on the table.
2 to make an egg
*The hen **laid** two eggs.*
see **lie**

layer something flat that lies over or under another surface

lazy not willing to work

lead[1] (*rhymes with* bed)
a soft gray metal that is very heavy

lead[2] (*rhymes with* seed)
1 to go in front of other people to show them where to go or what to do
*He will **lead** us to safety.*
2 to be in charge of a group
*Christian **led** the horses to the barn.*

3 a strap fastened to a dog's collar so that you can control it

leader a person or animal that leads

leaf one of the flat green parts that grow on trees and other plants

league (leeg)
a group of teams that play against one another

leak to have a hole or crack that liquid or gas can get through
*This kettle **leaks**.*

lean 1 to bend your body toward something
2 to rest against something
3 to make something slope
4 not fat
***lean** meat*

leap to jump
*I **leaped** up as if I'd been stung.*

leap year a year with an extra day in it, the 29th of February. A leap year comes once every four years.

learn 1 to find out about something
2 to find out how to do something
*He **learned** to read last year.*

leash a dog's lead

least 1 less than all the others
*the **least** expensive bike*
2 the smallest amount

leather a strong material made from the skins of animals
leather shoes

leave 1 to go from a person or place
2 to let something stay where it is
*I've **left** my book at home.*

leaves more than one leaf

led *see* **lead**²

ledge a narrow shelf like the one that sticks out under a window

leek a long, white vegetable with green leaves that tastes like an onion

left 1 on the side opposite the right
2 see **leave**

left-handed using the left hand to write and do other important things, because you find it easier than using the right hand

leg 1 a part of the body from the hip to the foot
2 one of the things a chair or table stands on
3 part of a journey
*We finished the first **leg** of our trip today.*

legend a story that was first told long ago by people who thought it was true. Most legends are not entirely true.

leisure time when you can do

what you want to do, because you do not have to work

lemon 1 a pale yellow fruit with a sour taste
2 the pale yellow colour of lemons

lemonade a drink made from lemons, sugar, and water

lend to let someone have something of yours for a short time
*I **lent** you my bike yesterday.*

length 1 how long something is
2 a piece of rope or cloth

lengthen 1 to make longer
2 to get longer

lens a curved piece of glass or plastic that makes light go where it is needed. Cameras and telescopes have lenses.

leopard a big wild cat found in Africa and Asia. It has yellow fur with black spots on it.

leotard (lee-a-tard)
a piece of clothing that is like very tight stockings that go up to the waist

less 1 not as much
2 take away
*Six **less** four is two, 6-4 = 2.*

lessen 1 to make less
2 to become less

lesson 1 the time when someone is teaching you

2 something that you have to learn

let to allow

let's a short form for *let us*

letter 1 one of the signs used for writing words, such as a, b, or c
2 a written message sent to another person

lettuce a vegetable with green leaves, eaten in salads and sandwiches

level flat and smooth
level ground

lever a bar that is pulled down to lift something heavy or make a machine work

liar someone who tells lies

library a building or room where a lot of books are kept for people to use

librarian a helpful person who is in charge of a library

licence a printed paper that says that you can do, own, or use something
a dog **licence**

lick to move the tongue over something

lid the top or cover of something

lie 1 to rest with the body flat as it is in bed
I **lay** *down and went to sleep.*
The cat has **lain** *here all night.*

He has been **lying** *here.*
2 to say something that is not true
You **lied** *to me yesterday.*
He was **lying***.*
3 something you say that is not true
He tells **lies***.*

life the time between birth and death
Do cats have nine **lives***?*

lifeboat a boat that goes out to sea in bad weather to save people's lives

lift 1 to move upwards
2 to pick up something

light 1 the power that makes things able to be seen. Light comes from the sun, the stars, flames, and lamps.
2 to start something burning
I struck a match and **lit** *the fire.*
3 pale
light blue
4 having a small mass
as **light** *as a feather*

listen 1 to make lighter
2 to get lighter

lighthouse a tower with a bright light that warns ships of rocks or other dangers

lightning the bright light that flashes in the sky during a thunderstorm

like 1 to think someone or something is pleasant

2 nearly the same as another person or thing

lighthouse

likely expected to happen or to be true

lilac 1 a tree with a lot of white or purple flowers that smell very sweet
2 a pale purple colour

lily a flower with trumpet-shaped blooms

lima bean a round flat bean eaten as a vegetable

limb a leg, arm, or wing

lime 1 a white powder used in making cement
2 a pale green fruit like a lemon
3 a kind of tree

limit a line or point that people cannot or should not pass
a speed **limit**

limp 1 to walk with difficulty

because there is something wrong with your leg or foot
2 not stiff

line 1 a long, thin mark like this

_____

2 a row of people or things

linen strong cloth used for making sheets and tablecloths

liner a big ship for taking people on long journeys

linger to be slow to leave

lining cloth covering the insides of clothes or curtains

link 1 to join things together
2 one of the rings in a chain

linoleum a stiff, shiny covering for the floor

lion a large, light brown wild cat found in Africa and India

lioness a female lion

lip one of the two edges of the mouth

lipstick something that looks like a crayon and is used for colouring lips

liquid anything that is like water, oil, or milk

list a group of things or names written down one after the other
a shopping **list**

listen to pay attention in order to hear something

lit see **light**

109

litre, liter (*rhymes with* Peter)
a measure of liquid
*a **litre** of paint*

litter 1 paper, empty packages, bottles, and other rubbish dropped or left lying about
2 all the young animals born to the same mother at the same time

little 1 not big
*a **little** boy*
2 not much
***little** time*

live[1] (*rhymes with* give)
1 to have your life
2 to have your home in a place

live[2] (*rhymes with* dive)
alive

lively full of life and energy
*a **lively** dance, a **lively** horse*

lives (*rhymes with* dives)
more than one life

lizard a creature with skin like a snake and four legs

llama a South American animal that looks like a camel without a hump

load 1 something that is carried
2 to put things on to something that will carry them

3 to put information into a computer
4 to put bullets into a gun

loaf bread in the shape it was baked in
*two **loaves***

loan 1 anything that is lent to someone
2 to lend something to another person

loaves more than one loaf

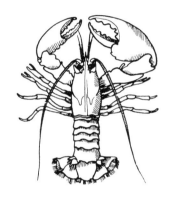

lobster a sea creature with a shell, two large claws, eight legs, and a tail

local belonging to one place
***local** radio*

lock 1 to fasten with a key
2 a fastening for a door, gate, or box that is opened with a key
3 a piece of hair

locomotive the engine that pulls a train

locust an insect that flies about in large groups destroying plants by eating them

log a piece of a tree

loiter to stand about with nothing to do

lollipop a big candy on the end of a stick

lonely 1 sad because your are on your own
2 far from others
a **lonely** house

lonesome see **lonely**

long 1 measuring a large distance from one end to the other
a **long** road
2 taking a lot of time
a **long** holiday
3 to long for to want something very much

look 1 to use your eyes
2 to try to find something
3 to seem
You **look** sad.

lookout 1 a person who watches for danger
A **lookout** stands at the front of the boat.
2 a place where you can stand to see a great distance
We stopped at a **lookout** in Cape Breton.
3 a careful watch
Mom kept a **lookout** for the truck.

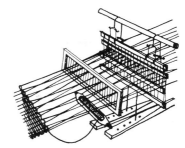

loom a machine for weaving cloth

loop a ring made in rope, wire, thread, or ribbon

loose (looss)
1 not tight
2 not fixed to anything

loosen 1 to make looser
2 to become looser

loot things that have been stolen

lose (looz)
1 to be without something you once had
2 to be without something, because you cannot find it
I've **lost** my coat.
3 to be beaten in a game
We **lost** last Saturday's match.

loss the losing of something

lot 1 plenty
There are a **lot** of fish in the Grand Banks.
2 a piece of land
Our house is on a small **lot**.

lotion a liquid that is put on the skin

loud 1 very easy to hear
2 noisy

loudspeaker 1 a machine that makes sound louder
2 the part of a television, radio, or record-player that the sound comes from

lounge 1 a room with comfortable chairs in it
2 a chair on which you can stretch out your whole body
3 to relax

love to like very much

lovely 1 beautiful
a **lovely** face
2 pleasing
a **lovely** idea

low not high

loyal always true to your friends

luck the way things happen that have not been planned

lucky having good luck
a **lucky** charm

luggage bags, boxes, and suitcases taken by someone on a journey

lukewarm only just warm

lullaby a song that is sung to send a baby to sleep

lumber wood that is cut to special sizes for building

lump 1 a solid piece with no clear shape
a **lump** of clay
2 a swelling

lunar having to do with the moon
The spaceship returned with **lunar** rocks.

lunch a meal eaten in the middle of the day

lung one of the parts inside the body used for breathing

lurch to lean suddenly to one side

lurk to wait where you cannot be seen

luxury something expensive that you like very much but do not really need

lying see **lie**

lynx a small wildcat found in North America

Mm

macaroni little tube-like pieces of food made from flour, eggs, water, and salt. Macaroni is a pasta.

machine something with several parts that work together to do a job
a washing-**machine**

machine-gun a gun that can keep firing very quickly for a long time

machinery machines or the parts of machines

mad 1 a word for angry
Tanya gets **mad** at her brother sometimes.
2 having a very strong liking
Scott is **mad** about motorbikes.

madam a word sometimes used when speaking politely to a woman, instead of using her name

made see **make**

magazine a kind of thin book that comes out every week or month with different stories and pictures in it

maggot a tiny worm that comes from an egg laid by a fly

magic the power to do wonderful things or clever tricks that people cannot usually do

magician someone who knows a lot about magic and uses it

magnet a metal bar that can make pieces of iron or steel come and stick to it

magnificent 1 very grand
a **magnificent** palace
2 splendid
a **magnificent** present

magnify to make something look bigger
a **magnifying** glass

magpie a black and white bird

maid a girl or woman who is a servant

mail letters, cards, and parcels sent through the post office

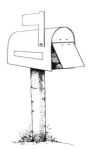

mail box a box used only for mail

main the most important
*a **main** road*

majesty a word used when
speaking to a king or queen
*Your **Majesty***

make 1 to get something new
by putting other things together
*I've **made** a boat out of paper
and wood.*
2 to cause something to
happen
*You **made** me do this last time.*

make-believe pretending
*Sally and Tony like to **make-
believe** they are forest rangers.*

make-up cream, lipstick, and
powder put on the face to make
it look different

male any person or animal that
can become a father

mall a special area where
people may walk but no
vehicles are allowed

mama see **mom**

mammal any animal that has a
backbone, a warm body, and
can feed its babies with its own
milk

man a fully grown male
*two **men***

manage 1 to be in charge of a
store or factory
2 to be able to do something
although it is difficult

mane the long hair along a
horse's back or on a lion's head
and neck

manger (mane-jer)
a long, narrow container that
horses and cattle can eat from
when they are in the stable

mangle to cut up or crush
something badly

manner the way something
happens or is done

manners your behaviour toward
other people

mansion a big, important house

mantle the shelf above a
fireplace

manufacture 1 to make large
numbers of the same thing
2 to make something from
other material

many a large number of people
or things

map a diagram that shows a part
of the world

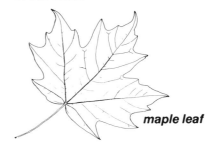

maple leaf

maple a kind of tree

The leaf of the **maple** *tree is one of Canada's symbols.*

marble 1 a small, glass ball used in some games
2 a kind of smooth stone used for building or making statues

march to walk like soldiers on parade

mare a female horse

margarine a food that looks and tastes like butter, but is not made from milk

margin the empty space between the edge of a page and the writing or pictures

marigold a bright orange or yellow flower

marine found in the sea. Seals, walruses, and whales are marine animals

mark 1 a stain, spot, or line that spoils something
dirty **marks**
2 a sign or number put on a piece of work to show how good or bad it is
Valerie has high **marks** *on her report card.*
3 a check or a line to show something is important or has been completed
Put a **mark** *beside the name of everyone who remembers to close the door.*

marker 1 a piece of material or sign put near something to draw attention to it
The police set out **markers** *around the hole in the road.*
2 a pen that can have ink of many different colours

market a group of stalls selling food and other things. Markets are usually held in the open air.

marmalade jam made from oranges or lemons

maroon 1 a very dark red colour
2 to leave someone in a wild and lonely place without any way of escaping from it

marriage a wedding

marry to become someone's husband or wife

marsh a piece of very wet ground

marvellous wonderful
a **marvellous** *story*

mash to crush something to make it soft and get rid of the lumps
mashed *potato*

mask a covering worn on the face

mass a large number or amount
masses *of flowers*

massive very big

mast a tall pole that holds up a ship's sails or a flag

master a man who is in charge

match 1 a small, thin stick that gives a flame when rubbed on something rough
2 a game played between two sides
3 to be the same as another thing or like it in some way

material 1 anything used for making something else
2 wool, cotton, or anything else that is woven and used for making clothes or covers

mathematics, math finding out about numbers, measurement, and shapes

matter 1 to be important
2 something you need to think about or do
a *serious* matter
3 What's the matter? What is wrong?
4 any solid material

mattress the thick, soft part of a bed

may 1 can
May I go out to play?
2 will perhaps
It *may* rain later.
It *might* rain later.

maybe a word used for "possibly"

mayor the person in charge of the local government in a town or city

maze a set of lines or paths that twist and turn so much that it is very easy to lose the way

me see **I**

meadow a field covered with grass

meal the food eaten at breakfast, lunch, dinner, tea, or supper

mean 1 not generous
2 to plan in your mind
I *meant* to tell him, but I forgot.
3 to have a meaning

meaning what someone wants to say with the words she is using

meant (*rhymes with* tent) see **mean**

meanwhile during the time something else is happening

measles an illness that makes red spots come on the skin

measure to find out how big something is

measurement how much something measures

meat the flesh of animals used as food

mechanical worked by or like machinery
a *mechanical* toy

medal a piece of metal in the shape of a coin, star, or cross

medal

given to someone very brave or very good at something
*a gold **medal***

medallist someone who has won a medal

meddle to take part in something that has nothing to do with you

medicine liquid or tablets that a sick person has to take in order to get better

medium of middle size

meek gentle and not proud

meet 1 to come together
2 to come face to face with another person
*I **met** her in town yesterday.*

meeting a group of people who have come together to talk about something or to listen to someone

melon a large, juicy fruit with a yellow or green skin

melt to change into a liquid

when heated. Ice melts.

member someone who belongs to a group

memory 1 the ability to remember
2 anything that is remembered

men more than one man

mend to make a damaged thing as useful as it was before

mention to speak of something or someone when you are talking about other things

menu a list of the different kinds of food you can choose for your meal in a restaurant

mercy being kind to someone instead of punishing him
*Show **mercy** to the prisoners.*

merry happy and gay

mess things that are untidy, dirty, or mixed up

message words that you send to someone to tell him something when you cannot speak to him yourself

messenger someone who takes a message to someone else

met see **meet**

metal something hard that melts when it is very hot. Gold, silver, iron, and tin are all kinds of metal.

meteor a small piece of rock or metal that moves through space and burns up when it gets near the earth

meteorite a lump of rock or metal that has fallen through space and landed on the earth

meter a machine that measures how much of something has been used
gas **meters**

metre, meter a measure of length
1000 **m** = 1 km

method the way you choose to do something

microphone a machine that changes sound into electricity so that it can be sent along wires to loudspeakers

microscope an instrument that makes it possible to see very tiny things by making them look much bigger

midday twelve o'clock in the day

middle the part of something that is the same distance from all its sides or edges or from both its ends

midget someone who is unusually small

midnight twelve o'clock at night

might see **may**

mild gentle

milk a white liquid that mothers and some female animals feed their babies with. People can drink the milk that comes from cows.

mill 1 a kind of factory
2 a place with machinery for making wheat into flour

millionaire someone who has very much money

mime to tell someone something by using actions not words

mimic to copy someone in order to make fun of him

mind 1 the power to think, feel, and understand
Your work shows that you have an active **mind**.
2 to look after
I'll **mind** the baby.
3 to be worried or upset by something

*Do you **mind** missing the party?*

mine 1 a place where people work to dig coal, metal, jewels, and other valuable things out of the ground
2 a bomb hidden in the ground or the sea to blow up things that come close to it
3 belonging to me
*That's **mine**.*

miner someone who works down a mine

mineral any useful or valuable rock that people get out of the ground

mingle to mix

miniature tiny, but just like something much bigger

minister 1 someone who is in charge of a church
2 an important person in the government

minnow a tiny fish found in rivers, streams, lakes, and ponds

minstrel a man who sang or played music to entertain people long ago

mint 1 a green plant used in cooking to give food flavour
2 a candy that tastes of mint
3 a place where coins are made

minus take away.
*Six **minus** two is four, 6 - 2 = 4.*

minute[1] (*min*-it)
sixty seconds

minute[2] (*my-newt*)
very tiny

miracle something wonderful that has happened, although it did not seem possible

mirage (mi-*rahj*)
a trick of the light that makes people see things that are not really there, such as pools of water in deserts

mirror a piece of glass in which you can see yourself

misbehave to be naughty

mischief silly or bad behaviour that gets you into trouble

mischievous likely to do silly or naughty things

miser someone who has a lot of money, but tries to spend as little as possible

miserable very unhappy

misery suffering
*great **misery***

misfortune something unlucky that happens

Miss a title used in front of the name of an unmarried woman

miss 1 to fail to hit, catch, see, hear, or find something
2 to be sad because someone is not with you

missile an object that is thrown or shot through the air

mission an important job that someone is sent away to do

mist damp air that is difficult to see through

mistake something you have done or thought that is wrong
*spelling **mistakes***

mistletoe a plant with green leaves and white berries in the winter. It is used to decorate houses at Christmas

misunderstand to get the wrong idea about something
You **misunderstood** what I said.

mitt a glove for playing baseball

mitten a kind of glove with two parts, one for the thumb and one for all the fingers

mix to stir or shake different things together to make one thing

mixture something made of different things mixed together

moan 1 to make a soft sound that shows you are in pain or trouble
2 to grumble

moat a ditch dug around a castle and usually filled with water

mobile able to move about

moccasin a soft shoe or slipper with no heels or laces

mock 1 to make fun of someone
2 not real
a **mock** battle

model 1 a small copy of something
2 someone whose job is to wear new clothes to show people what they look like

modern of the kind that is usual now
a **modern** house

moist damp

mole a small gray, furry animal that digs holes under the ground

mom a word for mother

moment a very small amount of time

monarch a ruler who is a king, queen, emperor, or empress

monastery a house where monks live and work

money the coins and pieces of paper people give when they buy things and receive when they sell things

mongrel a dog that is a mixture of different kinds of dogs

monitor 1 a television screen **2** a boy or girl with a special job to do at school

monk one of a group of men who live together and obey rules because of the religion they believe in

monkey an animal with hands, feet it can use like hands, long arms, and a tail

monster a large, frightening animal in stories

monorail a kind of train that runs on only one track

month a measure of time. There are twelve months in a year.

monument a statue or building made so that people will remember someone or something

mood the way you feel
*in a good **mood***

moon the satellite that goes around the earth and shines in the sky at night. Sometimes it looks completely round and sometimes like part of a circle.

moor to tie up a boat so that it will not float away

more 1 a larger number or amount **2** again
*I'll tell you once **more**.*

morning the time from the beginning of the day until the middle of the day

mortar a mixture of sand, cement, and water, used in building to stick bricks together

mosaic a picture made from coloured pieces of paper, glass, stone, or wood.

moss a plant that grows in damp places

most 1 more than any other **2** very
*She was **most** kind*

moth an insect with large, coloured wings. Moths usually fly around at night

mother a female parent

motocross a kind of motorcycle very good for riding where there are no roads

motor the part inside a car or machine that makes it move

motorbike a bicycle with an engine

motorcycle a very large and powerful motorbike

mould (*rhymes with* old)
1 furry stuff that sometimes grows on food that has spoiled
2 a container for making things like jelly or plaster set in the shape that is wanted

mound a pile of earth

mount to get on to a horse or bicycle so that you can ride it

mountain a very high hill

mountain lion see **cougar**

mouse a very small animal with a long tail and a pointed nose
three blind ***mice***

moustache hair that grows above a man's top lip

mouth the part of the face that opens for eating and speaking

move 1 to take from one place to another
2 to go from one place to another

movement moving
a sudden ***movement***

movie a film shown in a theatre

mow to cut grass or hay

Mr. a title used before the name of a man

Mrs. a title used before the name of a woman who is married

Ms a title used before the name of a woman

much a lot of something

mud wet soil

muddle to mix things up and make a mess of something

muffin a bread that is small and round
a bran ***muffin***

mule an animal that is half horse and half donkey

multiply to make something a number of times bigger.
Two ***multiplied*** *by four is eight,*
$2 \times 4 = 8$.

mumble to speak in a way that is not clear so that it is difficult to hear your words

mumps an illness that makes the sides of the face swell

munch to chew noisily

murder to kill someone on purpose

murmur to speak in a very soft, low voice

muscle one of the parts inside the body that become tight or loose in order to make the body move

museum a place where a lot of

interesting things are kept for people to go and see

mushroom a kind of fungus that people can eat

music the sounds made by someone singing or playing a musical instrument

musical 1 having to do with music
musical instruments
2 good at music

musk ox an animal like a bison but smaller. It has large curved horns and lives in the far North.

must have to
I *must* go now.

mustard a yellow powder or liquid used to give food a strong flavour

mutiny an attack made by soldiers or sailors against the officers in charge of them

mutter to murmur or grumble

mutton meat from a sheep

muzzle 1 an animal's nose and mouth
2 a cover put over an animal's nose and mouth so that it cannot bite

my belonging to me
Bo is **my** dog.

myself 1 I and no one else
2 by myself on my own

mysterious strange and puzzling

mystery something strange and puzzling that has happened

Nn

nag 1 to keep telling someone that you are not pleased and that she ought to behave differently
2 a worn-out and very old horse

nail 1 a small piece of metal with a sharp point, used for fastening pieces of wood together
2 see **fingernail**

naked without any clothes or covering

name what you call someone or something

nap a short sleep

napkin a small cloth or paper for wiping your mouth and fingers when you eat

narrow not wide, with very little room between the walls or sides

nasty 1 not kind
a **nasty** person
2 not pleasant
a **nasty** day

nation a country and the people who live in it

national belonging to one country
Canada's **national** hockey team has players from many provinces.

native someone born or something grown in a certain place
a **native** of Newfoundland

natural 1 made by nature, not by people or machines
2 normal
It is **natural** for birds to fly

nature 1 plants, animals, the sea, and everything else in the world that was not made by people
2 what a person or animal is really like

naughty badly behaved

navigate to make sure that a ship, airplane, or car is going in the right direction

navy 1 a group of ships and the people trained to use them for fighting
2 dark blue

near not far away, also **nearby**

nearly not quite
nearly 3 o'clock, **nearly** $100
nearly there

neat tidy

necessary needed very much

neck the part of the body that joins the head to the shoulders

necklace beads, jewels, or a chain worn around the neck

nectar a sweet liquid inside flowers. Bees collect nectar to make honey.

necktie a piece of narrow cloth worn around the neck and underneath a shirt collar

need 1 to be without something that you ought to have

2 to have to do something
*I **need** to go to the dentist.*

necktie

needle 1 a very thin, pointed
piece of metal. Needles used
for sewing have holes in them
2 one of a pair of rods used for
knitting
3 a very thin, pointed leaf. Pine
trees have needles.

neglect to leave something
alone and not look after it

neigh to make the noise a horse
makes

neighbour, neighbor
someone who lives next door or
near to you

neither not either
***Neither** of the twins has a bike.*

nephew the son of a brother or
sister

nerve 1 one of the small parts
inside the body that carry
messages to and from the

brain, so that the body can feel
and move
2 brave or calm behaviour
when there is danger
*Don't lose your **nerve.***

nervous 1 afraid and excited
because of something you
have to do
2 easily frightened
*a **nervous** animal*

nest a cosy place made by birds,
mice, and some other animals
for their babies

nestle to curl up comfortably

net 1 the cage at both ends of a
hockey rink or soccer field
2 a material like a web

network a system of connected
things
*A **network** of radio stations.*

never not ever

new 1 just bought or made
*a **new** bike*

2 different
*my **new** school*

newborn a person or animal that has just been born

news words that tell you about something that has just happened

newspaper large sheets of paper folded together, with the news printed on them. Most newspapers come out every day.

newt a small creature that lives near water and has four legs and a long tail

next the nearest

nibble to eat something by biting off a little at a time. Rabbits nibble carrots.

nice pleasant

nickname a name you call someone instead of his real name
*Wayne Gretzky's **nickname** is the Great Gretzky.*

niece the daughter of a brother or sister

night the time when it is dark

nightingale a small, brown bird that sings at night

nightmare a frightening dream

nimble able to move quickly and easily

nip to bite someone or squeeze his skin between the thumb and finger

noble brave and generous

nobody no person

noël a French word for Christmas

nod 1 to shake your head up and down, meaning 'yes'
2 to let your head fall forward in sleep
*Millie began to **nod** her head.*

noise sound that is loud and often not pleasant

none not any or not one

non-fiction stories that are true

nonsense something that does not mean anything

noodle a strip of dough. Noodles are pasta.

noon twelve o'clock in the day

no one no person

normal usual or ordinary

north the direction to your left when you face east

northern from the north or in the north

nose the part of the face that is used for breathing and smelling

nostril one of the two holes at the end of the nose for taking in air

notch a mark like a V, cut into something

note 1 a short letter
2 one sound in music

notebook a book with blank pages so that you can write things in it

nothing not anything

notice 1 to see something and think about it
2 something fixed to a wall for you to read

noun any word that tells you what someone or something is called. Air, Ann, speed, Quebec, and chair are all nouns.

nourish to feed someone well

nourishment proper food that you eat

novel a long story that is made up. A novel is the only story in a whole book

novelty something new or unusual

now at this time

nowhere not anywhere

nozzle the part at the end of a piece of pipe where a spray of

liquid or powder comes out

nude without any clothes

nudge to push someone with your elbow to make her notice something

nugget a lump of gold

nuisance someone or something that causes trouble

numb not able to feel anything

number the word or sign that tells you how many. 1, two, and 3 are numbers.

numerous many

nun one of a group of women who live together and follow rules because of the religion they believe in

nurse 1 someone whose job is to look after people who are ill or hurt
2 to hold carefully in the arms

nursery a place where very

young children go to play and
be looked after

nut 1 a kind of fruit found inside
a hard shell
2 a short piece of metal that is
screwed on to the end of a bolt
to make it firmer

nutrition 1 food
2 the way the body uses food

nylon a strong thin material for
making things like clothes and
rope

oak a large tree with seeds or
nuts called acorns

oar a long pole with a flat part at
one end, used for rowing a boat

oasis a place with water and
trees in a desert

oath a serious promise

oats a plant grown by farmers. Its
seed is used for feeding
animals and for making food
such as porridge.

obedient willing to do what you
are told to do

obey to do what you are told to
do

object[1] (*ob*-ject)
anything that can be seen or
touched

object[2] (ob-*ject*)
to say that you do not like or
agree with something

oblige 1 to help and please
someone
2 to have to do something

oblong a shape like a circle that
has been stretched.

observe to watch carefully

obstacle something that is in
the way

obstinate not willing to change
your ideas even though they
might be wrong

obstruct to be in the way so that
something cannot get past

obtain to get

obvious very easy to see or
understand

occasion the time when
something happens
a special **occasion**

occasionally sometimes

occupation any job or hobby

occupy 1 to live in something
2 to keep someone busy and
interested

occur 1 to happen
2 to come into your mind
An idea **occurred** *to me.*

ocean a big sea

o'clock by the clock
one **o'clock**

octopus a sea creature with eight arms

odd 1 strange
*an **odd** person*
2 not even
*Five is an **odd** number.*
3 not alike
***odd** shoes*

odour, odor a smell

of 1 from
*My puck is made **of** rubber.*
2 about
*The story **of** the king is exciting.*
3 named
*Abby lives in the city **of** Victoria.*

off 1 away
*They ran **off**.*
2 not on
*Turn the tap **off**.*

offend to hurt someone's feelings

offensive nasty and very annoying
*an **offensive** smell*

offer 1 to hold out something so that another person can take it if he wants it
2 to say that you are willing to do something

office a room with desks and telephones, where people work

officer someone in the army, navy, or air force, who is in charge of others

official a person who is important in a place or at a particular time

often many times

ogre a make-believe giant who is very big and ugly

oil a thick, slippery liquid. Oil is put in machines to make them work better and is burned to make heat. Another kind of oil is used in cooking.

ointment a cream for putting on sore skin or cuts

O.K. 1 all right
***O.K.** I will play now.*
2 correct
*Your spelling is **O.K.** now.*
The word is also written OK and okay.

old 1 born or made a long time ago
2 not new

old-fashioned of the kind that was usual a long time ago
***old-fashioned** clothes*

omelette eggs that are mixed together and fried with other food like onions and green peppers

omit to leave out

on 1 touching the surface
*The puck is **on** the ice.*
2 through
*We heard the game **on** the radio.*
3 a member of
*Maria is **on** the team.*
4 beside
*Our house in **on** a ravine.*
5 in use
*Is the TV **on**?*
6 at the time of
*We played our game **on** Monday.*

once 1 one time
*In baseball a batter may bat more than **once**.*
2 at one time
*Christmas comes **once** a year.*

one 1 a number
2 any thing or person
***One** hopes for good weather.*
3 the same
*All the horses ran in **one** direction.*

onion a round, white vegetable with a very strong flavour

only 1 no more than
***only** two cakes*
2 one by itself
*the **only** one left*

onto on the top of
*Jill jumped **onto** the wagon.*

onward, onwards forward
***onward,** soldiers!*

ooze to come slowly through a hole or small opening. Blood oozes from small cuts.

open 1 not closed
2 to make open

opening a hole or space in something

opera a kind of play in which everyone sings instead of speaks

operation 1 something done by doctors to a sick person's body to make it healthy again
2 the working of a machine

opinion what you think of something

opportunity a good chance to do something

opposite 1 facing
2 something that is as different as possible from another thing. Hot is the opposite of cold.

optician someone who makes or sells eyeglasses

orange 1 a round, juicy fruit with thick peel and white seeds
2 the colour of this fruit

orbit the path in space of something moving around the sun or a planet. The moon is in orbit around the earth.

orchard a place where a lot of fruit trees grow

orchestra a group of people who play musical instruments together

ordeal a time when you have to put up with pain or trouble

order 1 to tell someone to do something
2 to ask for something to be brought to you
3 in order properly arranged

ordinary not special in any way

ore rock with metal in it

organ a large musical instrument with pedals and pipes, and black and white keys like a piano.

organize 1 to get people working together to do something
2 to plan and arrange things like parties, concerts, or holidays
*She is good at **organizing** games.*

original 1 made first, before any others
2 new and not copied from anywhere
*an **original** idea*

ostrich

ornament something put in a place to make it look pretty

orphan a child whose mother and father are dead

ostrich a very large bird that cannot fly and has long legs

other not the same as this
*The **other** candies were better.*

otherwise or else

otter a furry animal that lives near water. Otters have long tails.

ought should
*I **ought** to brush my teeth.*

ourselves 1 we and no one else
2 by ourselves on our own

out 1 not in
2 not burning
*The fire has gone **out**.*

outfit 1 clothes that are worn together
2 a set of things needed for doing something

outing a day or afternoon out somewhere
*an **outing** to the zoo*

outline a line around the edge of something, that shows its shape

outside 1 not inside
2 the surface or edges of something

outstanding unusually good
***outstanding** work*

oval the shape of an egg

oven the space inside a stove, where food can be baked or roasted

over 1 above or covering
2 finished
*Playtime is **over**.*
3 remaining
*Is there any food left **over**?*
4 more than
*There were **over** 40,000 at the game.*

overall something worn over other clothes to keep them clean

overboard over the side of a boat into the water
*Man **overboard**!*

overflow to come over the sides of a container, because there is too much in it

overhead 1 above the head
***overhead** wires*
2 in the sky above

*a plane flying **overhead***

overtake to catch up and pass someone

overturn to push or knock something over

owe to have to pay money to someone

owl a bird with large eyes that hunts smaller animals at night

own 1 to have something that belongs to you
2 to say that you were the one who did something
*to **own** up*
3 mine and no one else's
*my **own***
4 by myself
*on my **own***

ox a large animal kept for pulling carts
*two **oxen***

oxygen the gas in the air that everyone needs to breathe in order to stay alive

oyster a sea creature that lives inside a pair of shells

pace 1 one step
2 how quickly something happens or moves

pack 1 to put things into a box, bag, or suitcase in order to move them or store them
2 a group of wolves or other animals
3 a group of Brownies or Cubs
4 a set of cards used in games

package a parcel

packet a small parcel

pad 1 sheets of writing paper joined together along one edge so that you can tear a sheet off when you need it
2 soft material folded up into a kind of cushion to protect something
3 to walk softly

paddle 1 a thin piece of wood with a flat part at the end, used to make a canoe move
2 see **joystick**

padlock a lock joined to something by a metal loop

page one side of a piece of paper that is part of a book

pageant (paj-ent)
a kind of play with many people in it. A pageant is usually about something that happened long ago.

paid see **pay**

pail a bucket

pain the feeling that you have when part of your body is damaged or sick

paint 1 a coloured liquid put on the surface of something to colour it
2 to use paint to colour something

painting a picture that has been painted

pair two people, animals, or things that belong together

pajamas loose clothing you wear while you are in bed

palace a very large house where a king, or queen, or some other very important person lives

pale 1 almost white
a **pale** face
2 light
a **pale** blue sky

palm 1 the inside of the hand between the fingers and wrist
2 a tropical tree with large leaves and no branches

pamper to treat a person or animal very well

pan 1 a metal dish for frying food on a stove

2 to look for gold in the gravel bottom of a river or stream

pancake flour, milk, and eggs mixed together and fried

panda an animal found in China. Giant pandas look like large black and white bears.

pane a piece of glass in a window

panel 1 a long, flat piece of wood or metal that is part of a door, wall, or piece of furniture **2** a group of people who discuss something so that others can learn from them

panic sudden fear that cannot be controlled

pansy a small plant with a brightly coloured flower

pant to take the short, quick breaths you need after running a lot or working hard

panther a kind of wild cat like a cougar found in Africa and Asia

pantomime a kind of play, in which the actors do not speak but tell a story by movements and dances

pantry a small room where food is kept

pants a piece of clothing for the lower part of the body

papa see **Dad**

paper 1 wet rags, straw, or tiny pieces of wood pressed and dried into very thin sheets. Paper is used for making books and wrapping up things. **2** a newspaper

parable a story told in order to teach people something

parachute a large piece of cloth that opens up like an umbrella when a cord is pulled. It is tied to someone's back so that she can jump out of an airplane and float safely down to the ground.

parade people marching along, while other people watch them

paragraph a group of sentences in a story that are all about one idea
*The first **paragraph** in the story of Joe Batt is about his childhood.*

parallel lines straight lines that are always the same distance from each other

paralysed not able to move or feel anything

parcel something wrapped up ready to be carried or mailed

pardon to forgive

parent 1 a person who has a child
2 an animal that has young ones

park 1 a large garden where anyone can walk or play
2 to leave a car somewhere for a time until it is needed again

parka a warm winter coat with a hood to cover your head

parliament the group of people that makes the laws of a country
*In Canada, the **Parliament** is made up of the House of Commons and the Senate.*

parrot a brightly coloured bird

that can learn to repeat things that are said to it

parsley a green plant used in cooking to give a stronger flavour to food

parsnip a pale yellow vegetable with a sweet taste

part anything that belongs to something bigger

particle a very tiny piece
***particles** of dust*

particular only this one and no other
*This **particular** one is my favourite.*

partner one of a pair of people who dance together, who play on the same side in a game, or who work together

partridge a wild bird, brown and black in colour, slightly smaller than a chicken

party a group of people enjoying themselves together
*a Christmas **party***

pass 1 to go by
2 to give someone something he wants, but cannot reach himself
*Please **pass** the salt.*
3 to be successful in a test
*She's **passed** her driving test.*

passage 1 a way through
2 a corridor

passenger anyone travelling in a bus, train, ship, or airplane, except the driver and crew

passport special papers printed by the government that a person has to have in order to go into another country

past 1 the time that has gone
2 up to and further than something
Go **past** the school.

pasta a mixture of flour, water, eggs, and salt to make dough for things like macaroni and noodles

paste a wet mixture used for sticking paper to things

pastime something you do in your free time

pastor a minister or priest in charge of a church

pastry 1 cakes, cookies, and sweet buns
2 a mixture of flour, fat, and water rolled flat and baked

pasture land covered in grass that cattle, sheep, or horses can eat

patch 1 a small piece of material put over something to mend it or protect it
2 a small piece of ground

path a very narrow way that you can go along to get somewhere

patience the ability to be patient

patient 1 someone who is ill and being looked after by a doctor
2 able to bear pain or trouble
3 able to wait for a long time without getting angry

patio an area just outside a house where people can sit or have parties in nice weather

patrol to keep walking around a place to look after it

patter to make the light, tapping sound rain makes against a window

pattern 1 a set of lines and shapes drawn on something to make it look pretty
2 anything that people copy in order to make something
a dress **pattern**

pause to stop for a very short time

pavement a hard surface such as concrete on a road

paw an animal's foot

pay to give money in return for something
I **paid** for lunch last time.

pea a tiny, round, green vegetable that grows inside a pod

peace 1 a time free from war
2 a time of quiet and rest

peaceful quiet

peach a round, soft, juicy fruit with a large stone and a thin, yellow skin
peaches and cream

peacock a large bird with very long, brightly coloured tail feathers that it can spread out like a fan

peak 1 the top of a mountain **2** the part of a cap that sticks out in front

peal to make a loud, ringing sound

peanut a tiny, round nut that grows in a pod in the ground

pear a juicy fruit that is narrow where the stalk is and at the end is round like a ball. Pears are yellow and look like a light bulb.

pearl a small, shiny white ball found inside the shells of some oysters. Pearls are used for making valuable jewellery.

pebble a small, round stone

peck to use the beak to pick up food or push at something

peculiar strange
a *peculiar* taste

pedal a part that is pressed with the foot to make something work. A bicycle has two pedals.

pedestrian someone who is walking

peek to look quickly or secretly

peel the skin on some fruit and vegetables

peep 1 the short high sound made by baby birds
2 see **peek**

pelican a bird with a very large beak that lives on water or near to it

pellet a tiny ball of wet paper, metal, food, or medicine

pelt 1 an animal's hair or skin **2** to throw a lot of things at someone

pen 1 a stick-like tool for writing **2** a small closed place for animals like pigs

penalty a kind of punishment

pencil a thin wooden stick used for writing and drawing

pendant something hung around the neck on a long chain or string

pendulum a rod with a weight hanging from its end so that it swings back and forth. Some clocks are worked by pendulums.

penetrate to make or find a way through something

penguin a sea bird that cannot fly and uses its short, stiff wings for swimming

peninsula a large finger of land that sticks out into water
*Part of the province of Nova Scotia is a **peninsula.***

penknife a small knife that folds

up so that you can carry it with you safely

penny a coin
*She counted out six **pennies.***

people men, women, and children

pep energy

pepper a powder used to give food a stronger flavour

peppermint a candy with a strong mint flavour

perch 1 anything that a bird rests on when it is not flying **2** to sit on the edge of something, like a bird on a branch

percolator a coffee-pot that makes coffee by forcing boiling water through ground-up coffee

percussion instrument any musical instrument that is banged, hit, or shaken. Drums, cymbals, and tambourines are percussion instruments.

perfect so good that it cannot be made any better

perform to do something in front of an audience

performance something done in front of an audience

perfume a liquid with a very sweet smell

perhaps possibly
Perhaps it will rain tomorrow.

peril danger

perimeter the distance around the edge of something

period 1 any length of time, such as period in a hockey game
2 a mark of punctuation to show the end of a sentence

periscope a special tube with mirrors that helps people to look at something that is out of sight

perish to die

permanent able to last for a very long time without changing

permission words that say something is allowed

permit to allow

persist to carry on doing something no matter what happens

person a man, woman, or child

personal belonging to one person and therefore private
*That drawer holds all my **personal** notes.*

persuade to get someone to agree to something

pest any person or animal that causes a lot of trouble

pester to keep worrying someone by asking questions

pesticide a poison for insects or animals like rats

pet 1 an animal that is kept for pleasure
2 favourite
*Do you have a **pet** teacher?*

petal one of the separate, coloured parts of a flower

petition a request for something signed by very many people
*People in the village took up a **petition** for a new fire truck.*

pew one of the long wooden seats in a church

phase one of the stages in a series
*The full moon is one of the **phases** it goes through.*

phone *short for* telephone

photo, photograph a picture taken with a camera and printed on paper

phrase a group of words, such as *in the green field*

physical having to do with the body
***physical** education*

piano a large musical instrument with white and black keys that are pressed with the fingers

pick 1 to choose
2 to take something up from where it is
***Pick** up that paper.*
3 to take flowers or fruits from plants and trees
4 see **pickaxe**

pickaxe, pick a heavy tool with a long handle, for breaking up very hard ground

pickles cucumbers stored in vinegar

picnic a meal eaten in the open air away from home

picture a painting, drawing, or photograph

pie meat or fruit covered with pastry and baked

piece a part of something

pier something long that is built out into the sea for people to walk on

pierce to make a hole through something

pigeon a bird with a large body and a small head

pig a farm animal raised for its meat called pork

pile a number of things put on top of one another

pilgrim someone who makes a journey to a holy place

pill a small, round piece of medicine

pillar a wooden or stone post that helps to hold up a building

pillow the cushion that you rest your head on in bed

pilot 1 someone who steers an airplane
2 someone who steers a ship in narrow, difficult places

pimple a small, round swelling on the skin

pin 1 a piece of wood or metal used to hold something together
2 a piece of jewellery
*Mom wears a **pin** that was given to her by Dad.*
3 one of the objects that you try to knock over with a ball in bowling

pincers a tool for holding something tightly

pinch to squeeze skin between the thumb and finger in order to hurt someone

pine a tree with cones for its seeds and clusters of leaves that look like green needles

pineapple a large fruit that grows in hot countries. It has stiff, pointed leaves and a thick skin covered in lumps.

pink a colour

pioneer 1 one of the first people to go and live in a new country **2** someone who is the first to do something

pipe 1 a tube for taking gas or water somewhere **2** a tube with a small bowl at one end, used for smoking tobacco

pirate someone on a ship, who attacks and robs other ships

pistol a small gun

pitch 1 to throw **2** a black, sticky liquid made from tar **3** to put up a tent

pitchfork a tool like a very large fork, for lifting hay

pity the feeling you have when you are sorry that someone is in pain or trouble

pivot a point that things swing from, spin around, or balance on. Wheels and see-saws have pivots.

pizza a large round flat piece of dough with tomato sauce and cheese on it and sometimes other food as well

pizza

placard a notice

place any space where something belongs

plague a dangerous illness that spreads very quickly

plaid (plad) a design made by crossing stripes *Cecile wore a **plaid** skirt.*

plain 1 not decorated **2** not pretty **3** easy to understand **4** a large area of flat ground

plan 1 to decide what is going to be done **2** a map of a building or town

plane 1 *short for* airplane **2** a tool for making wood smooth **3** a tall tree with large leaves

planet any of the stars in space that move around the sun. Earth is a planet. So is Mars.

planetarium a special building where you can learn about space and the stars and planets

plank a long, flat piece of wood

plant 1 anything that grows out of the ground. Trees, bushes, and flowers are all plants.
2 to put seeds and plants into the ground so they will grow

plantation a very large farm where crops like cotton are grown

plaster a soft mixture that goes hard when it dries. Plaster is used on walls of buildings, for mending broken bones, and for making models.

plastic light and strong material that is made in factories and used for making all kinds of things, such as plastic bowls, plastic bags, plastic toys.

plasticine something soft and coloured that you can make into different shapes with your hands

plate a flat dish for food

plateau a large piece of flat land that is high in the hills or mountains

platform 1 a small stage
2 the place in a station where people wait beside the tracks for a train

play 1 to be in a game
2 to make music with a musical instrument
3 a story that is acted out on stage

player a person who takes a part on a team or at any kind of game

playground a place out of doors where children can play

playing-card one of a set of cards used in some games

plaza 1 a shopping centre
2 a public square in a city or town

plead to beg for something that you want very much

pleasant pleasing
a **pleasant** holiday

please 1 to make someone happy
2 the polite word you use when you are asking for something
Please may I have another muffin?

pleasure the feeling people have when they are pleased

pleat a flat fold made in the material of a dress, skirt, or kilt

plenty 1 a lot of something
2 more than enough

pliers a tool for holding something tightly or for bending or breaking wire

plod to walk slowly and heavily

plot 1 to plan secretly
   2 a small piece of ground

plough, plow (*rhymes with* cow)
a machine used on farms for digging and turning over the soil

pluck 1 to pull a feather, flower, or fruit from the place where it is growing
   2 to pull at something and let it go quickly. People play guitars by plucking the strings.

plucky brave

plug 1 a part joined to a lamp or machine by wire. It fits into a place in a wall where electric power can come into it.
   2 a round piece of rubber or metal that fits into a hole. It stops water running out of a bathtub or sink.

plum a juicy fruit with a stone in it

plumber (plummer)
someone who puts in and mends taps and water pipes

plume a large feather

plump fat

plunder to rob a person or place of many things by force

plunge 1 to jump suddenly into water
   2 to put something suddenly into water

plural any word when it is written differently to show that it means more than one. Cakes, children, ladies, mice, and monkeys are all plurals.

plus add
*Three **plus** three is six, 3+3 = 6.*

plywood a kind of wood made from thin sheets of wood glued together

pneumonia (new-monia)
a serious illness that makes it painful to breathe

poach 1 to cook an egg in boiling water or steam without its shell
   2 to hunt animals that are on someone else's land

pocket a part like a small bag, sewn into some clothes

pod 1 a long seed case that grows on some plants. Peas grow inside pods.

2 an arrangement of rooms so that people can move around easily and work together if they wish

poem a piece of writing with a special rhythm. Poems are usually written in short lines.

poet someone who writes poetry

poetry poems

point 1 the sharp end of things such as pins and pencils
2 a mark scored in a game
3 to show where something is by holding out your finger toward it
4 to aim a weapon

pointed with a point at the end

poison any liquid, powder, or plant that will kill or harm you if you swallow it

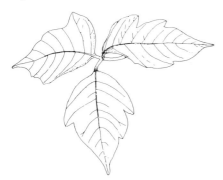

poison ivy a plant with white berries and leaves in groups of three. Poison ivy will cause a rash if you touch it.

poisonous likely to harm you because it contains poison
poisonous berries

poke to push hard with the end of your finger or a stick

poker a metal rod for poking a fire

polar bear a very large, white bear that lives in the Arctic

pole 1 a long, round stick of wood or metal
2 either of the two ends of a magnet
3 North Pole the place that is the farthest north in the world
4 South Pole the place that is the farthest south in the world

police the people whose job is to catch criminals and make sure that the law is kept. There are thousands of policemen and policewomen in Canada.

polish to rub the surface of something to make it shine

polite having good manners
a *polite* boy

poll 1 a count of people to ask their opinion about something
2 the place where people go to vote in an election

pollen the yellow powder inside a flower

poncho a piece of cloth with a hole in the middle for the head, worn over clothes

poncho

pond a very small lake

ponder to think about something carefully

pony a small horse

poodle a kind of dog with curly hair often cut very short on some parts of its body

pool a small area of water

poor 1 having very little money
*a **poor** family*
2 bad
poor work, poor crops

popcorn kernels of corn that have puffed up and burst when they were heated

poplar a tall, straight tree

poppy a bright red flower

popular liked by a lot of people

population the number of people who live in a place

porch a small place with a roof, in front of the door of a building

porcupine a small wild animal

covered with sharp, hard hair like needles

pork meat from a pig

porpoise a sea animal like a small whale

porridge a hot food made from oats boiled in water

port a large place where ships can stay safely in the water when they are not at sea

portable able to be carried about
*a **portable** television set*

porter someone whose job is to carry other people's luggage at places like hotels and railway stations

portion the part or amount given to you

portrait a picture of a person

position 1 the place where something is or should be
2 how the body and its parts are arranged
*a sitting **position***

positive completely sure

possess to own

possible able to happen or to be done

post 1 an upright pole fixed in the ground
2 to send a letter, parcel, or card

postal code a system of numbers and letters put on mail to speed delivery

postcard a piece of card that you can write a message on and mail

poster a large notice for everyone to read

post office a place that sells stamps and deals with letters and parcels

postpone to put off until later

potato a vegetable dug out of the ground
baked **potatoes**

potion a drink with medicine or poison in it

pottery cups, plates, and other things made of baked clay

pouch 1 a small bag
2 a kind of pocket that some animals have in their skin. Hamsters have pouches inside their cheeks.

poultry birds kept for their meat and eggs

pounce to attack something by jumping on it suddenly

pound 1 to beat very hard with the fists
2 to crush something by hitting it very hard

pour 1 to hold a container so that liquid runs out of it quickly
2 to rain hard

pout to stick out your lips when you are not pleased

powder anything that is very dry and made up of many separate tiny bits, like flour or dust

power 1 the ability to do something
2 strength

powerful very strong or important

practical 1 able to do useful things
2 likely to be useful
a **practical** idea

practice something you keep doing in order to get better at it
piano **practice**

practise to do something over and over again in order to get better at doing it

prairie a very large area of flat ground covered in grass

praise to say that someone or something is very good

prance to jump about in a very lively way
a **prancing** horse

pray to talk to God

prayer talking to God

preach to speak to other people just as in a sermon in church

precious very valuable
a **precious** jewel

precipice a very steep part of a mountain or rock

prefer to like one person or thing more than another person or thing

prefix a letter, syllable, or word put on the beginning of a word to change the meaning of it. Happy becomes 'unhappy' when the prefix 'un' is added.

pregnant expecting a baby

prehistoric belonging to a time very long ago
prehistoric animals

preparations things that are done to get ready for something

prepare to get something ready

present[1] (prez-ent)
1 something given to someone
2 the time now
Our teacher is away at **present.**
3 here
All **present** and correct, sir!

present[2] (pri-zent)
to give someone a prize or gift in front of other people

presently soon

preserve 1 to keep safe
2 to do things to food so that it will not spoil

president 1 someone chosen to rule a country that does not have a king or queen
2 someone who is the leader of a company or club

press 1 to push hard on something
2 to make something flat or smooth by pushing hard on it

pressure 1 pressing on something
2 how much one thing is pressing on another

pretend to make it seem that something not true is true
He **pretended** he was ill.

pretty pleasant to look at
a **pretty** girl, a **pretty** dress

prevent to stop something from happening

previous coming before this one
the **previous** week

prey 1 any animal hunted by another animal
2 a bird that hunts and eats other animals
a bird of **prey**

price very valuable

prick to make a tiny hole in something

pride the feeling people have when they are proud

priest someone who leads people in their religion

Prime Minister the most important person in some governments

prince the son of a king or queen, or the husband of a queen

princess 1 the daughter of a king or queen
2 the wife of a prince

principal most important or chief

principle an important rule

print 1 to write with letters that are not joined together
2 to use a machine that presses words and pictures on to paper. Books, newspapers, and magazines are printed.

prison a place where criminals are kept as a punishment

prisoner 1 someone who has been captured
2 someone in prison

private 1 not open to everyone
a **private** road
2 not known by other people
a **private** thought

prize something that is won

probable likely to be true or to happen

problem something that is difficult to understand or to answer

proceed to go on

procession a group of people moving in a long line

prod to push something with the end of a finger or stick

produce 1 to make
2 to bring something out so that it can be seen

producer the person in charge of presenting a play

profit money got by selling something for more than it cost to buy or make

program, programme 1 a talk, play, or show on the radio or television
2 a list for people in an audience telling them about what they will see or hear
3 instructions to a computer

progress 1 moving forward
2 getting better

prohibit to say that people must do something

project 1 finding out as much as you can about something interesting and writing about it
a **project** on butterflies
2 a plan

promise to say that you will certainly do or not do something

*He's always **promising** us a reward.*

prompt done right away

prong one of the thin, pointed parts on the end of a fork

pronounce to say a sound or word in a certain way

proof something that shows that an idea is true

prop 1 a long piece of wood or metal put underneath something to support it
2 to support one thing by leaning it against another thing
*The ladder was **propped** up against the wall.*

propel to drive forward

propeller a set of blades that spin around. Propellers are fixed to airplanes, helicopters, and ships to make them move.

proper correct
*in the **proper** place*

property things that belong to someone

prophet someone who tells people what is going to happen

prose writing or speaking that is not poetry

prosecute to make someone go to court so that he can be punished if he has done wrong
*Trespassers will be **prosecuted.***

prosper to become successful or rich

protect to keep safe from danger

protection something that protects

protest to say or show that you think what someone else is saying or doing it wrong

proud 1 full of the idea that you are better or more important than you really are
2 very pleased because you or someone belonging to you has done well
*He is **proud** of his sister.*

prove to show that an idea is true

proverb something often said in order to help people, such as 'A stitch in time saves nine.'

provide to give something that is needed

prowl to move about like an animal looking for something to kill and eat

prune 1 a dried plum
2 to cut parts off a tree or bush

pry to force something loose

psalm (sahm) one of the hymns in the Bible

public 1 all the people
2 open to everyone

publish to prepare books, magazines, and newspapers for sale.

pudding something sweet made to be eaten after the main part of a meal

puddle a small pool of water

puff 1 a small amount of breath, wind, or smoke
2 to blow out puffs of air
3 puffed out of breath

puffin a sea bird with a large orange and blue beak

pull to get hold of something and make it come toward you

pulley a wheel with rope around it, used for lifting heavy things

pulp anything that has been made soft and wet
*fruit **pulp**, paper **pulp***

pulpit the high wooden desk in a church, where someone stands to talk to the people

pulse the throbbing that can be felt at the wrist as the blood is pumped around inside the body

pump 1 a machine that pushes liquid or air through pipes
2 to push air or liquid into something
***Pump** up that flat tire.*

pumpkin a very large, round fruit with a hard yellow skin

punch 1 to hit with the fist
2 a tool for making holes in paper or leather

punctual exactly on time

punctuation marks such as commas and periods put into a piece of writing to make it easier to read

puncture a hole in a tire or other object which holds air or water

punish to make someone who has done wrong suffer

punishment something done to punish someone

pupil 1 someone who has a teacher
2 the black spot at the centre of the eye

puppet 1 a kind of doll whose head and limbs can be moved by strings and rods
2 a kind of doll with a body like

a glove, so that you can move its head and arms with your fingers

puppy a very young dog

purchase to buy

pure with nothing else mixed with it

purple a colour

purpose what someone means to do

purr to make the sound a cat makes when it is very pleased

purse a small bag for holding money

pursue to run after someone and try to catch him

push to use your hands to move something away from you

put to move something into a place
*I **put** the dishes away yesterday.*

putty something soft and sticky that sets hard, used for fixing glass into windows

puzzle 1 a game or question that is difficult to solve and makes you think a lot
2 to make someone think very hard to find the answer
*a **puzzling** question*

pyjamas see **pajamas**

pylon a metal tower that holds up high electric cables

pylon

pyramid a large, stone building made by the ancient Egyptians to hold the body of a dead king or queen. Pyramids have sloping sides that meet in a point at the top.

quack to make the sound a duck makes

quaint unusual but pleasant
*a **quaint** cottage*

quake to shake because you are very frightened

quality how good or bad something is

quantity an amount

quarrel to speak angrily to someone or fight with her because she does not agree with you

quarry 1 a place where people cut stone out of the ground so that it can be used for building **2** an animal that is being hunted

quarter one of the four equal parts something can be divided into. It can also be written as ¼.

quay (key) a place where ships can be loaded and unloaded

queen 1 a woman who has been crowned as ruler of a country **2** a king's wife

queer very strange a **queer** feeling

quench 1 to put an end to someone's thirst The tea **quenched** her thirst. **2** to use water to put out a fire

quest a long search

question something that you ask when you want to find out something

question mark a punctuation mark (?) put at the end of a written question

quick 1 done in less time than usual a **quick** snack **2** fast Be **quick!**

quiet 1 without any noise

2 not loud a **quiet** voice

quill a big feather from a bird's wing or tail

quilt a bed cover like a large, flat cushion

quit 1 to stop Please **quit** pushing now. **2** to leave Bernice **quit** her job yesterday.

quite 1 very I am **quite** certain. **2** almost but not entirely The picture was **quite** pretty.

quiver 1 to shake because you are very cold and frightened

2 a bag for carrying arrows

quiz a kind of game in which people try to answer a lot of questions in order to show how much they know two **quizzes**

quotation the exact words of a speaker

quotation marks punctuation marks (") that set off a speaker's words from other words in writing

Rr

rabbi a spiritual leader of Jewish people

rabbit a furry animal with long ears

raccoon a wild animal that hunts food at night. It is gray, brown and black, with a black face and black rings on its tail.

race a competition to find the fastest

rack a set of bars made into a shelf or something else that people can put things on
a luggage **rack**

racket 1 a kind of bat with a wooden or metal frame and string stretched across it in a criss-cross pattern
a tennis **racket**
2 a lot of loud noise

radiant 1 bright
radiant *sunshine*
2 looking very happy
a **radiant** *smile*

radiate to give out heat or light

radiator 1 a metal container or a set of pipes that gives out heat in a room
2 the part inside a car for keeping the engine cool

radio a machine that receives programs and messages sent through the air so that people can listen to them

radish a small, hard, round red vegetable, eaten raw

radius the distance from the centre of a circle to the edge
two **radii**

raffle a kind of sale held to raise money for something. People buy tickets with numbers on them and certain numbers win prizes.

raft something flat made of

pieces of wood joined together
and used instead of a boat

rafter one of the long, sloping
pieces of wood that hold up a
roof

rag a torn piece of cloth used for
rubbing or cleaning

rage great anger

raid a sudden attack on a place

rail 1 a bar or rod
2 a long metal bar that is part of
a railway track

railing 1 a fence made of metal
bars
2 a fence beside stairs

railroad 1 the tracks that a train
runs on
2 the company that owns and
runs trains

rain drops of water that fall from
the sky

rainbow the curved band of
different colours seen in the sky
when the sun shines through
the rain

raincoat a coat made of
waterproof material for keeping
you dry when it rains

raise 1 to lift up or make
something higher
2 to gather together the money
or people needed for something

raisin a dried grape

rake a tool used in the garden. It
has a long handle and a row of
short spikes

rally 1 a large number of people
who have come together for a
meeting
2 to begin to win again after
losing for a while
*The Blue Jays **rallied** for six
runs late in the game.*

ram 1 a male sheep
2 to push one thing very hard
into another thing

ramble a long walk in the
country

ran see **run**

ranch a large farm with a lot of
cattle or horses

random without any plan or aim

rang see **ring**

range 1 a large area with grass
for animals to eat
2 the distance that a vehicle,
bullet, or other thing can travel
3 a large stove for cooking
4 a group of mountains

rank 1 a title or job that shows how important someone is. The rank of general is higher than the rank of major.
2 a row of people

ransack to search everywhere for something and leave things looking very untidy

ransom money paid so that a prisoner can be set free

rap to knock quickly and loudly

rapid very quick

rare not often found. Pandas are rare animals.

rascal 1 a person who does not behave in a polite or gentle way
2 someone who is not honest

rash 1 done in a rush without any thought about what might happen
*a **rash** action*
2 red spots or patches that suddenly come on the skin
*a **measles** rash*

raspberry a soft, sweet, red berry

rat an animal that looks like a very large mouse

rate how quickly something happens or is done

rather 1 fairly
*It's **rather** cold.*
2 prefer to
*I'd **rather** have a steak.*

rattle 1 to make quick, hard noises by shaking something
2 a baby's toy that rattles

rattlesnake a poisonous North American snake that has hard rings at the end of its tail which make a noise when shaken

rave to talk in a very excited or enthusiastic way

raven a large, black bird

ravenous very hungry

ravine a low area between two higher ones. A ravine often has a stream running through it.

raw not cooked

ray a thin line of light
*the sun's **rays***

razor a very thin, sharp blade mostly used for shaving

reach 1 to stretch out the hand in order to touch something
*He **reached** for a pen.*
2 to arrive at a place

read (reed)
to be able to say and

understand words that are written down
*Can you **read** this?*
*I've **read** this before. (red)*

reader 1 a person who reads
*The **reader** of the story paused for a moment.*
2 a book with stories in it that children use to practise reading

ready 1 able and willing to do something at once
*Are you **ready** yet?*
2 fit to be used at once
*Everything is **ready**.*

real not a copy
*a **real** diamond*

realize to come to understand something clearly

really truly
*Is it **really** snowing?*

realm (*rhymes with* helm)
the land a king or queen rules

reap to cut down and gather in grain when it is ripe

rear 1 the back part of something
2 to care for children or young animals
3 to stand on the back legs and lift the front legs into the air, like a dog begging

reason anything that explains why something has happened

reasonable 1 fair
*a **reasonable** price*

2 sensible

rebel[1] (ri-*bell*)
to decide not to obey the people in charge
*The soldiers **rebelled**.*

rebel[2] (*reb*-el)
someone who rebels

recall to remember

receive to get something that has been given or sent to you

recent made or done a short time ago

recess the time of day when children in school are free to play or rest

recipe (resip-ee)
instructions that tell you how to cook something

recite to say a poem or something else that you have learned by heart

reckless likely to do silly or dangerous things. Reckless people do things without thinking or caring about what might happen.

reckon 1 to think something and feel sure it is right
2 to count or add up

recognize to know who someone is because you have seen her before

record 1 a flat, round piece of black plastic that makes music

or other sounds while it is turning around on a record-player
2 to put sound on the piece of round, black plastic, or on audio-tape so it can be heard
3 the best that has been done so far in a sport or hobby
*He broke the world **record** in that race.*
4 facts that are written down and kept

recorder a wooden musical instrument shaped like a tube, that you blow

record-player a machine that makes sounds come out of records

recover 1 to get better after being ill
2 to get something back that you have lost

recreation hobbies or games people like playing in their spare time

rectangle like a square but two sides opposite each other are longer than the other two

red a colour

reduce to make smaller or less

reed a plant with a strong stem that grows near water

reef a line of rocks just below or just above the surface of the sea

reek to have a strong smell that is not pleasant

reel 1 a round piece of wood or metal that thread, string, or film is wound around
2 a dance
3 to lose your balance because you feel dizzy

4 a device for winding up fishing line

refer 1 to say a little about something while talking about other things
*She **referred** to the game during her speech.*
2 to look in a book for information

referee someone who makes sure that the players in a game keep to the rules

reference book a book that gives you information. Dictionaries are reference books.

reflect 1 to send back light from a shiny surface. Water often reflects the light of the sun.
2 to show a picture of something, as a mirror does

reflection a picture seen in a mirror or water

refresh to make a tired person feel fresh and strong again
a refreshing drink

refreshments drinks and snacks

refrigerator a kind of metal cupboard that keeps food cold and fresh

refuse[1] (ri-*fuse*)
1 to say you will not do something you have been asked to do
2 to say you do not want what someone is offering you

refuse[2] (*ref*-yooss) garbage

regard to think of someone or something in a certain way

regiment a large, organized group of soldiers

region a part of a country or the world

register an important book with a list of names and addresses in it
a school register

regret the feeling you have when you are sorry about something

regular 1 usual
2 always happening at certain times
regular meals

rehearsal a practice for a concert or play

rehearse to practise something before it is done in front of an audience

reign 1 to be king or queen
2 the time when someone is king or queen

reindeer a kind of deer that lives in very cold countries

reins the two long straps used for guiding a horse

rejoice to be very happy about something

relation a relative

relative someone in the same family as you

relax to rest the body by letting it become less stiff

relay race a race between teams in which each person does part of the distance

release to set someone free

relent to be less angry than you were going to be

reliable able to be trusted
a reliable person

relic something very old that was left by people who lived long ago

relief the feeling you have when you are no longer in trouble, pain, or danger

relieved happy because you are no longer in trouble, pain, or danger

religion what people believe and the way they worship

reluctant not willing to do something

rely to trust someone or something to help
*The blind man **relied** on his dog.*

remain 1 to stay
2 to be left behind

remainder what is left over

remark to say something that you have thought or noticed

remarkable so unusual that you remember it easily
a ***remarkable*** story

remedy something that cures an illness or a problem

remember to be able to bring something into your mind when you want to

remind to make or help someone remember something

remote far away

remove to take something away

rent an amount of money paid every week or month for the use of something that belongs to another person

repair to mend

repeat to say or do the same thing again

repent to be very sorry about something you have said or done

replace 1 to put something back
2 to take the place of another person or thing

reply to answer

report to tell or write news

represent 1 to speak or do things in place of another person or a group of people
2 to be a picture or model of something

reproach to tell someone how sad or angry you are that he has done wrong

reptile an animal with cold blood that creeps or crawls. Snakes, crocodiles, and tortoises are all reptiles.

reputation the things everyone says or thinks about a person

request to ask politely for something

require to need

rescue to save from danger

resemble to look or sound like another person or thing

reservation a special order for something to be kept for you until you arrive

*Mom made a **reservation** for five people at the restaurant.*

reserve to keep for later

reservoir a place where a very large amount of water is stored

resist to fight against something and not give way

resolve to decide

resource 1 a supply of something that is available for use
*Canada has many **resources** such as oil.*
2 a person who is ready to give special help
*We have a **resource** teacher in our school.*

respect the feeling you have for someone you like and admire

responsible in charge and likely to take the blame if anything goes wrong

rest 1 to lie down, lean against something, or sit without doing anything
2 the part that is left
3 the other people or things
*You stay, but the **rest** can go.*

restaurant a place where you can buy a meal and eat it

restore 1 to put something back
2 to make something as good as it was before

result 1 anything that happens because of other things that have happened
2 the score or marks at the end of a game, competition, or test

retire to stop working when you are old or ill
*My grandmother is **retiring** soon.*

retreat to go back because it is too dangerous to carry on

return 1 to come back to a place
2 to give something back

reveal to let something be seen or known

revenge a wish to hurt someone because he has hurt you or one of your friends

reverse 1 the opposite side or way
2 to go backwards in a car

revolt to say that you will not obey the people in charge

revolting so nasty that you feel sick

revolution a great struggle to change the government by force and put a new kind of government in its place

revolver a small gun that can be fired several times without having to be loaded again

reward a present given to someone because of something she has done

rhinoceros a very large, heavy animal found in Africa and Asia. Rhinoceroses have horns on their noses.

rhubarb a plant with pink stalks that are cooked and eaten

rhyme (rime)
a word that has the same sound at the end as another word. Bat and mat are rhymes and so are batter and matter.

rhythm (*ri*-them)
the pattern made in music or poetry by the strong and weak sounds

rib one of the curved bones above the waist

ribbon a strip of nylon, silk, or some other material

rice shiny white seeds that are cooked in liquid
rice pudding

rich having a lot of money
a *rich* miser

ridden see **ride**

riddle a question or puzzle that is a joke, such as
Why do Swiss cows have bells? Because their horns don't work.

ride 1 to sit on a horse or bicycle and control it as it moves along
*Have you **ridden** before?*
*I **rode** her pony yesterday.*
*Do you like **riding?***
2 to travel in a car, bus, or train

ridge a long, narrow part higher than the rest, like the line along the top of a roof

ridiculous so silly that people might laugh at it
*a **ridiculous** answer*

rifle a long gun that is held against the shoulder when it is fired

right 1 on the side opposite the left
2 correct
*the **right** answer*
3 fair
*It is not **right** to cheat.*
4 completely
*Turn it **right** around.*

right-handed using the right hand to write and do other important things, because you find it easier than using the left hand

rim the edge around the top of a round container or around the outside of a wheel

rind the skin on bacon, cheese, or fruit

ring 1 a circle
2 a circle of thin metal worn on the finger
3 to make a bell sound
*I've **rung** your bell twice.*

rink an area of ice or ground for skating on

rinse to wash something in clean water

riot a large group of people shouting and fighting

rip to tear

ripe ready to be gathered or eaten
***ripe** fruit*

ripen to become ripe

ripple a tiny movement on the surface of water

rise 1 to go upward
*The sun has already **risen.**
Prices are **rising.***
2 to get up
*They all **rose** as she came in.*

risk the chance of danger

rival someone trying to win the same prize as you are

river a large stream

road a way with a hard surface

made for people and traffic to go along

roam to move around without trying to get anywhere

roar to make the loud, deep sound a lion makes

roast to cook meat or vegetables inside the oven

robber someone who steals

robbery taking things by force from other people
*a bank **robbery***

robin a medium-sized bird, brown with a rust-coloured breast

robot a machine that can move and behave like a person

rock 1 something very hard and heavy that is part of the mountains, the hills, and the ground
2 to move gently back and forth

rocket 1 a firework joined to a stick. Rockets shoot high into the air when they are lit.
2 a tall, metal tube that is shot into space by hot gases rushing out of it at the bottom

rod a long, thin, round piece of wood or metal

rode see **ride**

rogue someone who is not completely honest

roll 1 a cylinder made by rolling

something up

2 a very small loaf of bread

3 to turn over and over like a ball moving along the ground

roller 1 a heavy cylinder rolled over things to make them flat or smooth

2 a small cylinder put in hair to curl it

roller skate a set of small wheels that fit under each shoe and make you able to move quickly and smoothly over the ground

rolling pin a wooden cylinder rolled over pastry to make it flat

roof the part that covers the top of a building

room 1 one of the spaces with walls around it inside a building. Bathrooms, kitchens, and dens are rooms.

2 enough space for something

roost the place where a bird rests at night

root the part of a plant that grows under the ground

rope a lot of strong threads twisted together

rose 1 a flower with a sweet smell and thorns on its stem

2 see **rise**

rosy coloured like a pink or red rose

rot to go soft or bad so that it

cannot be used. Fruit and wood rot.

rotten so soft or bad that it cannot be used

a **rotten** apple, **rotten** wood

rough 1 not smooth

rough wood

2 not gentle

a **rough** worker

3 not exact

a **rough** guess

round shaped like a circle or ball

roundup a gathering together of cattle or people.

rouse 1 to wake someone up

2 to make someone excited about something

route (root)

the way you have to go to get to a place

rove to travel around from place to place

row[1] (*rhymes with* toe)

1 people or things in a straight line

2 to use oars to make a boat move

row[2] (*rhymes with* how)

1 a quarrel

2 a lot of noise

royal belonging to a king or queen

the **royal** family

rubber 1 a strong material that stretches, bends, and bounces.

Rubber is used for making tires, balls, elastic bands, and many other things.
2 a piece of rubber for rubbing out pencil marks

rubbish 1 things that are not wanted or needed
2 nonsense
*You're talking **rubbish!***

ruby a red jewel

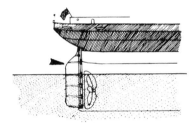

rudder a flat part fixed to the end of a ship or airplane and used to steer it

rude not polite

rugged (rug-id) rough and full of rocks
***rugged** countryside*

ruin 1 to spoil something completely
2 a building that has fallen down

rule 1 something that everyone ought to obey
2 to be in charge of a country and the people who live there
3 to draw a straight line with a ruler

ruler 1 someone who rules a country or empire
2 a strip of wood, metal, or plastic with straight edges, used for measuring and drawing straight lines

rumble to make the deep, heavy sound thunder makes

rumour, rumor something that a lot of people are saying, although it might not be true

run to use the legs to move quickly
*He saw the bull and **ran.***

rung 1 one of the short bars on a ladder
2 see **ring**

rural in the country
***Rural** life is very peaceful.*

rush 1 to move very quickly
2 a plant with a thin stem that grows in marshes

rust a rough, red surface that covers iron that has become damp or wet

rustle to make the light sounds dry leaves make when they are blown by the wind

rut a groove made in the ground by wheels going over it many times

rye a plant grown by farmers. Its seed is used for feeding animals and making some kinds of bread.

sack a large bag made of strong, rough material
*a **sack** of potatoes*

sacred very holy

sacrifice to give up something very important

sad feeling unhappy

saddle a seat put on a horse's back so that you can ride it

safari a journey made by people in order to hunt or look at lions and other wild animals

safe 1 free from danger
2 a strong box where money or valuable things can be kept from thieves

safety a time or place free from danger
*The fireman carried her to **safety.***

safety belt a special belt that you wear in a car to keep from being hurt in an accident. It is also called seat belt.

sag to go down in the middle because something heavy is pressing on it
*The chair **sagged** when he sat down.*

said see **say**

sail 1 a large piece of strong cloth joined to a boat. The wind blows into the sail and makes the boat move.
2 to travel in a boat

sailor a member of a ship's crew

saint a very holy person
***St.** Nicholas*

sake benefit or good
*Jimmy turned down the radio for the **sake** of the others who were asleep.*

salad a mixture of vegetables eaten raw or cold

salary money paid to someone each month for work done

sale 1 the selling of things
2 a time when things in a store are sold at reduced prices

salesperson a person who sells

salmon a large fish with pink flesh

salt a white powder put on food to make it taste better

salute to touch your forehead with your hand, as soldiers do to show respect

same not different in any way
*My dress is the **same** as yours.*

sample a small amount that shows what something is like
*free **samples***

sand the tiny bits of rock that cover deserts, beaches and other ground

sandal a kind of light shoe with straps that go around the foot

sandwich two slices of bread and butter with a different food between them
a ham **sandwich**

sang see **sing**

sank see **sink**

sap the liquid inside a plant or tree

sapling a young tree

sardine a small sea fish

sash a strip of material tied around the waist of a dress

sat see **sit**

satchel a bag worn over the shoulder or on the back for carrying things

satellite something that moves in space around Earth or another planet.
The moon is a **satellite** *of the Earth.*

satin smooth cloth that is very shiny on one side

satisfactory good enough
satisfactory *work*

satisfy to be good enough to please someone

sauce a thick liquid put on food to make it taste better

saucepan a metal pan with a handle and lid used for cooking things on top of a stove

saucer a kind of small plate for putting a cup on

sausage a skin tube stuffed with tiny pieces of meat and spices

savage wild and fierce
a **savage** *animal*

save 1 to free someone or something from danger
2 to keep something so that it can be used later
We're **saving** *wrapping paper.*

saw 1 a tool with a wide, thin blade that is moved back and forth across a piece of wood to cut it
2 to use a saw to cut a piece of wood
The wood was **sawn** *in two.*
I **sawed** *it in half yesterday.*
3 see **see**

sawdust a powder that comes from wood when it is cut with a saw

sawed, sawn see **saw**

say to use the voice to make words
He said he hadn't seen it.

saying something wise that is often said, such as 'A rolling stone gathers no moss.'

scab hard, brown skin that covers a cut or scrape while it is getting better

scabbard a cover for the blade of a sword

scaffolding planks fixed to poles and put around a building so that workers can stand on them while they are painting or repairing

scald to burn yourself with very hot liquid

scale 1 a weighing machine
2 a thin piece of skin or bone that covers the outside of animals such as fish and snakes

scalp the skin covering the top of the head where the hair grows

scamper to run about quickly. Small dogs scamper.

scar the mark left on the skin by a cut or burn after it has healed

scarce 1 not enough of something
Water is scarce in deserts.
2 not often seen or found

scare to frighten

Stop scaring me!

scarecrow something that looks like a person and is put in a field to frighten away birds so that they will not eat the crops

scarf a piece of material worn around the neck or head
two scarves

scarlet bright red

scatter to throw small things so that they fall in many different places

scene 1 the place where something happens
the scene of the crime
2 part of a play

scenery 1 painted curtains and screens put on a stage to make it look like another place
2 things such as hills, rivers, and trees that you can see around you when you are out in the country

scent 1 a pleasant smell
the scent of roses
2 an animal's smell
a fox's scent

scholarship money given to someone clever in order to help her to go on studying

school the place where children go to learn

schooner a ship with sails and at least two masts

schooner

science knowledge about the world that people get by studying things and testing ideas about the way they work

science-fiction make-believe stories about space and life on other planets

scientific having to do with science
a **scientific** experiment

scientist someone who studies science and does experiments to learn things

scissors a tool for cutting that has two blades joined together
a pair of **scissors**

scoff to make fun of something

scold to speak angrily to someone

scoop 1 a deep spoon for lifting up and measuring out food
2 to use a tool or your arms or hands to gather things together and lift them up

scooter 1 a toy with two wheels that is ridden. You stand on it with one foot and push the other foot against the ground to make it move.
2 a kind of motorbike with a very small engine

scorch to make something so hot that it turns brown

score 1 to get a goal or point in a game
2 the number of points or goals each side has at the end of the game
3 twenty
three **score** years and ten

scorn to show that you think someone or something is not worth bothering about

scout a person sent ahead to find out what the rest of the group must expect

Scout a boy who is a member of the Boy Scouts

scowl to make your face look unhappy and angry

scramble to use your hands and feet to climb up or down something

scrap 1 a small piece
2 rubbish

scrapbook a large book that has blank pages on which you can paste pictures and other things

scrape to rub with something rough or sharp

scratch 1 to damage something by rubbing your nails or a sharp point over it
2 to rub your skin to stop it itching

scrawl to write with big, untidy letters

scream to make a loud cry that shows that you are very frightened or in pain

screech to make a loud, shrill sound that is not pleasant. Some owls screech.

screen 1 a smooth surface on which movies or television programs are shown
2 a kind of thin wall or a set of curtains on rails, that can be moved about. Screens are used for hiding things or protecting people.

screw 1 a kind of nail that is put into a hole and twisted in order to fasten things tightly together
2 to turn or twist something

screwdriver a tool for turning a screw until it fits tightly into something

scribble to write or draw quickly and untidily

scripture a sacred book such as the Bible

scroll a book written on a long sheet of paper that is rolled up

scrub to rub something very hard with a brush dipped in soap and water

sculptor an artist who makes shapes and patterns in stone, wood, clay, or metal

scurry to run with fast, little steps. Mice scurry.

scuttle 1 to move quickly like a frightened mouse
2 a kind of bucket in which coal is kept

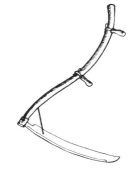

scythe (sythe) a tool with a long curved blade for cutting grass

sea a very large area of salt water

sea gull a kind of sea bird

seal 1 a furry animal that lives in the sea and on land
2 to close something by sticking two parts together. a **sealed** envelope

seam the line where two pieces of cloth are sewn together

search to look very carefully for something

searchlight a strong light that can be pointed in any direction

season 1 one of the four parts of the year. Spring, summer, autumn, and winter are the names of the seasons.
2 to put salt or pepper on food to make it taste better

seat a chair or stool or anything else on which people sit

seaweed a plant that grows in the sea

second 1 a very small measure for time
60 **seconds** = 1 minute
2 coming after the first
second prize

secret something that must be kept hidden from other people

secretary someone whose job is to type letters, answer the telephone, and arrange things in an office

section 1 a part of something

2 in western Canada a piece of land of a certain size

secure safe or firm

see to use your eyes to get to know something
I **saw** an accident this morning. Have you **seen** my cat anywhere?

seed a tiny thing put into the ground so that a plant can grow from it

seek to try to find
We **sought** for him everywhere, but could not find him

seem to make people think something is true or likely
He **seems** brave but he isn't.

seen see **see**

see-saw a plank balanced in the middle so that someone can sit on each end and make it go up and down.

seize to take hold of something suddenly

seldom not often
I **seldom** lose my temper.

select to choose

self everything in a person that makes him different from anyone else.

selfish only bothered about yourself and what you want

sell to give in return for money
I **sold** my bike yesterday.

semicircle half of a circle

send to make a person or thing go somewhere
She sent me a card last week.

senior older or more important

sensation 1 anything that you can feel happening to yourself
2 something very exciting that happens

sense 1 the power to see, hear, smell, feel, or taste
2 the ability to know what it is best to do or say

sensible wise
a sensible person
a sensible idea

sensitive easily hurt or offended
sensitive skin
a sensitive person

sent see **send**

sentence a group of words that belong together. A written sentence always begins with a capital letter and ends with a question mark like this ?, an exclamation mark like this !, or a period like this .
Is this a sentence? Yes, it is.

sentry a soldier who is guarding a building

separate not joined to anything

sequin one of the tiny, round, shiny things sewn on clothes to decorate them

sergeant a soldier or police officer who is in charge of other soldiers or police officers

serial a story told in parts
a television serial

series 1 a full set
a series of stamps
2 a number of things that are similar and come one after the other
a television series

serious 1 careful and thoughtful
a serious boy
2 not silly or funny
a serious talk
3 very bad
a serious accident

sermon a speech about religion, usually made from a pulpit

serpent a large snake

servant someone whose job is to work in someone else's house

serve 1 to work for someone
2 to sell things to people in a store
3 to give out food at a meal

serviette a square of cloth or paper for keeping you clean while you eat

session a time spent doing one thing

set 1 a group of people or things that belong together
a set of drums

2 to become solid or hard
*The jelly has **set** very quickly.*
3 to put
4 to set off to start
*They **set** off for home.*

settle 1 to become comfortable in a place and stay there
*We're **settling** down in our new home now.*
2 to decide

settlement a new town or village

settler a pioneer who goes to a new land and begins to make a living there

several more than a few but not a lot

severe 1 not kind or gentle
*a **severe** master*
2 very bad
*a **severe** cold*

sew (so)
to use a needle and thread to join pieces of cloth together
*He has **sewn** his badge on his jacket.*

sex one of the two groups, either male or female, to which all people and animals belong

shabby looking worn and faded
***shabby** clothes*

shack a rough hut

shade 1 a place that is darker and cooler than other places, because the light of the sun cannot get to it
2 how light or dark a colour is
3 to make part of a drawing darker than the rest

shadow the dark shape that you see on the wall or ground near something that is standing in the way of the light

shaft 1 a long, thin pole
*the **shaft** of an arrow*
2 a deep, narrow hole
*a mine **shaft***

shaggy with long, untidy hair
*a **shaggy** dog*

shake to move quickly up and down or from side to side
*I **shook** with fear, when I saw it. The trees were **shaken** by the wind.*

shall a word that shows something must happen in the future
*You **shall** come even if you are ill.*

shallow not deep
***shallow** water*

shame the feeling you have when you are upset because you have done wrong

shameful so bad that it brings you shame
***shameful** behaviour*

shampoo liquid soap used for washing hair

shamrock a small green plant

with each leaf like three small leaves joined together

shape the pattern that a line drawn around the outside of something makes. A ball has a round shape.

share 1 to make something into parts and give them out to other people
She **shared** the cake.
2 to use something that someone else is also using
Can I **share** your book?

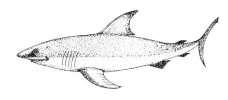

shark a large sea fish with sharp teeth

sharp 1 with an edge or point that can cut or make holes
a **sharp** knife
2 sudden
a **sharp** bend in the road
3 quick to notice things or learn
sharp eyes, a **sharp** student

shatter to break suddenly into tiny pieces

shave to cut hair from the skin to make it smooth

shawl a piece of cloth or knitting worn around the shoulders or wrapped around a baby

she a word instead of the name of a female person or animal

sheaf a bundle of grain tied together at harvest time
three **sheaves**

shears a tool like a very large pair of scissors for cutting plants or for clipping wool or hair from animals

sheath a cover for the sharp blade of a sword or knife

sheaves more than one sheaf

shed 1 a small hut
2 to let something fall. Trees shed leaves, people shed tears, and snakes shed their skins.

sheep an animal kept by farmers for its wool and meat
two **sheep**

sheer very steep because it is straight up and down like a wall
a **sheer** cliff

sheet 1 one of the large pieces of cloth put on a bed

2 a whole piece of paper, glass, or metal

shelf a long piece of wood fastened to a wall, for putting things on
two **shelves**

shell 1 the thin, hard part around an egg, a nut, and some kinds of animals, such as snails
2 a very large bullet that explodes when it hits something

shelter a place that protects people from wind, rain, cold, or danger
a bus **shelter**

shelves more than one shelf

shepherd someone whose job is to look after sheep

sheriff a person in charge of the law in a county or district

shield a large piece of metal, leather, or wood used for protecting someone. Soldiers long ago held shields in front of themselves while they were fighting.

shift to move something

shimmer to shine with a light that comes and goes, like the light of the sun on water

shin the front of the leg between the knee and ankle

shine 1 to give out light
2 to look very bright
He polished it until it **shone.**

shingle a flat, thin piece of material used to cover the roof of a building
We need many **shingles** for this big roof.

shiny with a surface that shines

ship a large boat that takes people or things on long journeys over the ocean

shipwreck a bad accident that destroys or sinks a ship while it is at sea

shirk to get out of doing something that you ought to do

shirt a piece of clothing for the top half of the body with sleeves, a collar, and buttons down the front

shiver to shake because you are cold or frightened

shock a big surprise that is not pleasant

shoe a strong covering for the foot, with a stiff sole and heel
leather **shoes**

shone see **shine**

shook see **shake**

shoot 1 to use a gun or a bow and arrow
2 to hurt or kill by shooting
3 to make something like a puck move toward a goal

shop 1 a place that people go into to buy things
2 to go to a store to buy something

shore the land along the edge of oceans, lakes, and rivers

short 1 not long
a **short** visit
2 not tall
a **short** person

shorthand a set of signs for writing words down as quickly as people say them

shorts trousers that only cover the top part of the legs

shot 1 see **shoot**
2 the firing of a gun

should ought to
You **should** be working.

shoulder the part of the body between the neck and arm

shout to speak very loudly

shove to push hard

shovel a kind of curved spade for lifting things such as coal or sand

show 1 to let something be seen
Show me your new bike.
2 to make something clear to someone
He's **shown** me how to do it.
3 singing, dancing, and acting done to entertain people
4 things that have been put together and arranged so that people can come and look at them

shower 1 a short fall of rain or snow
2 a lot of small things falling like rain
a **shower** of stones
3 to have a shower to stand under a spray of water and wash yourself

shown see **show**

shrank see **shrink**

shred a tiny strip or piece that has been cut, broken, or torn off something

shriek a short scream

shrill sounding very high and loud
a **shrill** whistle

shrimp a small sea creature with a shell

shrink to become smaller
It **shrank** when it was washed.
These jeans have **shrunk.**

shrivel to get very dry and curl

up at the edges like a dead leaf

shrub a bush

shrunk see **shrink**

shudder to shake suddenly because you are very cold or frightened

shuffle to drag your feet along the ground as you walk

shut to move a cover, lid, or door in order to block up an opening
*He **shut** the door and drove off.*

shutter 1 a wooden cover that fits over a window
2 a wooden cover that is fastened to the wall beside the window
3 the part inside a camera that opens to let in light as you take a photograph

shy 1 not willing to meet other people because you are afraid
2 easily frightened
*a **shy** animal*

sick ill

sickening very annoying
*How **sickening!***

side 1 one of the outer parts between the front and back of a person, animal, or thing
2 a flat surface
*A cube has six **sides.***
3 an edge
*A triangle has three **sides.***
4 a group playing or fighting against another group

sidewalk a paved pathway for people to walk on

sideways 1 with the side first
2 to one side

siege (seej)
a time when the enemy surrounds a town or castle so that people and things cannot get in or out

sigh to breathe out heavily to show you are feeling very sad or very happy

sight 1 the ability to see
2 something that is seen

sign 1 anything written, drawn, or done to tell or show people something
*road **signs***
2 to write your name in your own writing

signal a sound or movement that tells people something. Signals are used instead of words.

signature your name written by yourself in your own writing

silence a time when there is no sound at all

silent without any sound

silk very fine, shiny cloth made from threads spun by insects called silkworms

sill a ledge underneath a window

silly not clever or careful
*a **silly** person, a **silly** idea*

silver a valuable, shiny metal

similar like another person or thing
*Your dress is **similar** to mine.*

simple 1 easy
*a **simple** question*
2 plain
*a **simple** dress*
3 not complicated

since 1 from that time
2 because

sincere truly meant
***sincere** good wishes*

sing to use the voice to make a tune with sounds or words
*We have **sung** this before.*
*She **sang** a solo yesterday.*

singe to burn something slightly

single 1 only one
2 not married

singular only one person, place, or thing
*Book is a **singular** word meaning, 'one book'.*

sink 1 a place with taps where you can wash or get a drink
2 to go under water
*The ship **sank** last night.*
*It has **sunk.***
3 to go down

sip to drink a very small amount at a time

sir 1 a word used when speaking politely to a man, instead of using his name

2 a title given to knights
Sir Winston Churchill

siren a machine that makes a loud sound like a scream to warn people about something

sister a girl or woman who has the same parents as another person

sit to rest as you do when you are on a chair
*He **sat** on the chair and broke it.*
*Are you **sitting** comfortably?*

site the ground where something has been built or will be built

situation 1 the things that are happening to you
2 the place where something is

size 1 how big something is
2 the measurement something is made in
***size** ten shoes*

sizzle to make the noise bacon makes when it is being fried

skate 1 a steel blade joined to the sole of a boot and used for moving smoothly over ice
2 to move smoothly over ice or the ground wearing skates or roller-skates

skateboard a long piece of wood or plastic on wheels. You balance on it with both feet while it moves quickly over the ground.

skeleton the framework of

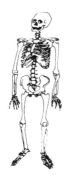

bones inside the body

sketch to draw quickly

ski a long piece of wood, metal, or plastic strapped to the foot for moving quickly and smoothly over snow
*a pair of **skis***
*We went **skiing** yesterday.*

skid to slide without meaning to

skill the ability to do something very well

skim 1 to take something off the top of something else
2 to move quickly over the surface of something and only just touch it

skin 1 the outer covering of the body
2 the outer covering of some fruits and vegetables

skip 1 to move lightly and quickly by hopping from one foot to the other
2 to jump over a rope that is turning

3 to miss on purpose
***Skip** the next page.*

skipper the person in charge of a ship or a team

skirt a piece of clothing that hangs down from the waist

skull the bony framework inside the head

skunk a black animal about the size of a large cat. It has white stripes on its tail and can give off a very bad smell.

sky the space overhead where the sun, moon, and stars can be seen

skyscraper a very tall, modern building

slab a flat, thick piece
*a **slab** of marble*

slack 1 not pulled tight
*a **slack** rope*
2 careless
***slack** work*
3 not busy
*a **slack** day*

slain see **slay**

slam to close something loudly

slanting in a line that is higher at one end than the other, like the side of a triangle or a hill

slap to hit with the flat part of your hand

slash to make long cuts in something

slaughter (slot-er)
the killing of many people or animals

slave someone who belongs to another person and has to work without wages

slay to kill
*The dragon was **slain.***
*St. George **slew** the dragon.*

sled see **sleigh**

sleek neat, smooth, and shiny
***sleek** hair*

sleep to close your eyes and rest completely, as you do every night
*I **slept** in a tent last night.*

sleet a mixture of rain and snow

sleeve the part of a coat, shirt, blouse, or sweater that covers the arm

slender thin
*a **slender** girl*

slept see **sleep**

slew see **slay**

slide 1 to move very quickly and smoothly over something
2 very slippery ground or a long, sloping piece of shiny metal on which people can slide
3 a small photograph that can be shown on a screen

slight 1 small
*a **slight** cold*
2 thin
*a very **slight** person*

slim thin
*a **slim** person*

slime wet, slippery stuff that is not pleasant

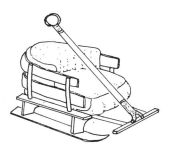

sleigh (*rhymes with* play)
something used for travelling over snow. Sleighs have strips of wood or metal instead of wheels

sling a piece of cloth wrapped around an injured arm and tied around the neck so that it supports the arm

slink to move in a secret way

179

because you are afraid or feel guilty about something
*The dog saw me and **slunk** away.*

slip 1 to slide without meaning to
2 to fall over
3 to go away quickly and quietly

slipper a soft, comfortable kind of shoe worn indoors

slippery with a very smooth surface so that it is difficult to get hold of or walk on

slit a long cut or narrow opening in something

slop to make a mess by letting liquid run over the edge of a container

slope ground that is like the side of a hill

slot a narrow opening for something like a coin to fit into

slouch to move, sit, or stand with the head and shoulders bent forward

slow 1 taking more time than usual
*a **slow** train*
2 showing a time that is earlier than the correct time. Watches and clocks are sometimes slow.

sludge thick sticky mud

slug a small creature like a snail without its shell

slumber sleep

slunk see **slink**

slush melting snow

sly clever at tricking people secretly

smack to hit with the flat part of the hand

small little
*a **small** dog*

smart 1 dressed well
2 neat and tidy
3 clever
4 to feel a stinging pain

smash to break into pieces with a loud noise

smear 1 to make a dirty mark by rubbing against something
2 to rub something over a surface

smell 1 to use the nose to find out about something
*I bent down and **smelled** the rose.*
2 anything that your nose is aware of

smile to make your face show that you are happy

smoke 1 blue or gray gas that floats up from a fire and looks like a cloud
2 to have a cigarette or pipe between the lips, take in the smoke from it, and breathe it out

smooth free from lumps or rough parts
*a **smooth** surface*

smother 1 to cover thickly
*a cake **smothered** in cream*
2 to cover someone's mouth and nose so that he cannot breathe

smoulder to burn slowly with a lot of smoke

smudge a dirty mark made by rubbing against something

smuggle to bring something into a country secretly without paying the tax that should be paid to the government

snack something you can eat quickly instead of a meal

snail a small creature that lives inside a shell. Snails are found on land and in water.

snake a creature with a long body and no legs. Some snakes can give poisonous bites.

snap 1 to break something suddenly by bending or stretching it
2 to bite suddenly

snapshot a photograph

snare a trap for catching animals

snarl to make the sound a dog makes when it is angry

snatch to take something quickly

sneak to move in a way so that you will not be seen or heard

sneer to speak or smile in an insulting way

sneeze to make a sudden noise as air rushes out of the nose
*I can't stop **sneezing.***

sniff to make a noise by suddenly taking in air through the nose

snip to cut a little bit off something

snob someone who only bothers with people that he thinks are as clever or important as he is

snooker a game played on a long table with rods and twenty-two small, coloured balls

snore to breathe very noisily while sleeping

snorkel a tube for someone to

breathe through while she is swimming under water

snout an animal's nose and mouth sticking out from the rest of its face. Pigs have snouts.

snow small, thin, white pieces of frozen water. Snow floats down from the sky when the weather is very cold.

snowball snow packed into a ball for throwing

snowdrop a small white flower that grows in early spring

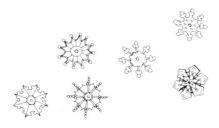

snowflake a single little bit of snow

snowman a statue made from snow that looks a little like a person

snowmobile a vehicle that travels over snow on skis. It is powered by a motor.

snub to show someone who is trying to be friendly that you do not want to be his friend

snug cosy

snuggle to curl up in a warm comfortable place

so 1 to such a degree
*Dolores was **so** hungry she ate everything.*
2 therefore
*It was raining **so** I went home.*
3 also
*I came and **so** did Peter.*
4 true
*Is that **so?***
4 more or less
*I will be home in ten minutes or **so**.*

soak to make something very wet

soap something used with water for washing

soar to move high into the air

soccer a game between two teams in which players try to kick a round ball into a net

sock a covering for the foot and part of the leg

socket the part that an electric light bulb or plug fits into

sofa a long, comfortable seat with a back, for more than one person

soft 1 not firm. Cotton and wet clay are soft.
2 not loud

softly gently

soggy wet through

soil the brown stuff on the ground, that plants grow in

solar having to do with the sun
the **solar** system

sold see **sell**

soldier a member of the army

sole 1 the flat part underneath a foot or shoe
2 a sea fish

solemn serious
a **solemn** face

solid 1 not hollow
2 firm. Liquids and gases are not solid.
solid food

solitary alone or lonely

solo something sung, played, danced, or done by one person

solution the answer to a puzzle or problem

solve to find the answer to a puzzle

some 1 a few
some candy
2 a certain amount of
some cake
3 a, an, or one
some animal

somebody a person

somehow in some way

someone a person

somersault (summer-salt)

1 a jump, turning head over heels in the air
2 a forward or backward roll on the ground

sometimes at some times

somewhere in some place or to some place

son a boy or man who is someone's child

song words that are sung

soon in a very short time from now

soot the black powder left behind by smoke

soothe to make someone who is upset feel calm
soothing words

sorcerer a person in fairy tales, who can do magic things

sore painful when it is touched
sore skin

sorrow a very sad feeling

sorry 1 sad about something that you wish you had not done
2 sad because of something that has happened to another person

sort 1 a kind
I like this **sort** best.
2 to arrange things into different groups

sought see **seek**

soul the part of a person that

cannot be seen but is believed to go on living after death

sound 1 anything that can be heard
2 to make a sound

soup a hot liquid made from meat or vegetables

sour 1 with the kind of taste lemons and vinegar have
2 not fresh
sour milk

source the place something has come from

south the direction to your right when you face east

southern from the south or in the south

souvenir (soo-ven-eer) something that you keep because it makes you think about a person or place

sovereign a ruler who is a king, queen, emperor, or empress

sow[1] (*rhymes with* toe)
to put seeds in the ground so that they will grow into plants
*The grain was **sown** in the spring.*

sow[2] (*rhymes with* how)
a female pig

space 1 the distance between things
2 a place with nothing in it
3 all the places beyond the earth, where the stars and planets are.
*Outer **space** is so vast that it cannot be measured.*

spaceship a machine that can carry people and things through space.

spade 1 a tool with a long handle and a short, wide blade for digging
2 a small, black spade printed on some playing-cards

spaghetti a food that looks like long pieces of string when it is cooked

span to reach from one side of something to the other, as a bridge does

spaniel a kind of dog with silky fur and long ears

spank to hit someone on the bottom

spare 1 not used but kept in case it is needed
*a **spare** tire*
2 to give up something so that someone else can have it
*Can you **spare** an apple please?*

spark 1 a tiny piece of burning stuff
2 a tiny flash

sparkle to shine with a lot of tiny flashes of bright light
sparkling jewels

sparkler a kind of firework that

sparkles. You can hold it in your hand while it burns.

sparrow a small, brown bird that is seen almost everywhere

spawn the eggs of frogs, fish, and some other creatures

speak to say something
*She **spoke** to me yesterday.*
*I've not **spoken** to him yet.*

spear a long pole or stick with a very sharp point, used as a weapon

special 1 different from any other kind
2 for one person or thing
*a **special** cake for my birthday*

specimen 1 a small amount of something that shows what the rest is like
2 an example of one kind of plant or animal

speck 1 a tiny mark
2 a tiny bit of dust

speckled with small, coloured spots. Some birds' eggs are speckled.

spectacles a pair of eye glasses

spectator someone watching a game or show

speech 1 the power of speaking
2 a talk given to a group of people

speed how quickly something

moves or happens

spell 1 to write a word correctly
*How is your name **spelled?***
2 magic words that make things happen

spend 1 to use money to pay for things
2 to pass time
*I **spent** yesterday at home.*

sphere (sfear)
the shape of a ball

spice part of a plant such as the berry or seed that is dried and used in cooking to give food a stronger flavour. Ginger and pepper are spices.

spider a small creature with eight legs that sometimes weaves webs to catch insects

spike a thin piece of metal with a sharp point

spill to let something fall out of a container
*The cat drank the **spilled** milk.*

spin 1 to turn around and around quickly
*I **spun** around until I was dizzy.*
2 to make thread by twisting long, thin pieces of wool or cotton together

spinach (spin-itch)
a vegetable with a lot of green leaves

spine 1 the long bone down from the centre of the back

2 a thorn

spinning wheel a machine for spinning thread. It is worked by the hand or foot.

spinster a woman who has not married

spiral 1 the shape of a line that keeps going around the same point in smaller and smaller or bigger and bigger curves
2 a spiral staircase a staircase that you go around and around as you climb up it

spire a tall, pointed part on top of a church tower

spirit 1 the part of a person that cannot be seen but is believed to go on living after death
2 a ghost
3 something that makes a person very brave and lively

spit to send drops of liquid out of the mouth

spiteful full of a wish to hurt someone by what you say or do

splash 1 to make drops of water fly about as they do when you jump into water
2 the noise you make when you jump into water

splendid 1 very good
a **splendid** holiday
2 looking very grand
a **splendid** costume

splint a straight piece of wood or metal that is tied to a broken arm or leg to hold it firm

splinter a sharp bit of wood, glass, or metal

split to break something into parts
He **split** the log with an axe.

spoil 1 to make something less good or useful than it was
2 to be too kind to a child so that he can always have what he wants
The little boy was very **spoiled.**

spoke 1 see **speak**
2 one of the wires or rods that

go from the centre of the wheel to the rim

spoken see **speak**

sponge something thick and soft with a lot of holes in it. Sponges soak up water and are used for washing.

spool a round piece of wood or metal that thread, string, or film is wound on

spoon the tool you use for eating soup and pudding

sport a game or something else that is usually done outside and exercises the body. Running, jumping, football, and hockey are all sports.

spot 1 a round mark
2 a small, round swelling on the skin
3 a place
4 to notice something
She **spotted** *the mistake at once.*

spotlight a strong light that can shine on one small area

spout the part of a container that is made like a pipe so that you can pour liquid out of it easily. Teapots and kettles have spouts.

sprain to twist the wrist and ankle so that it swells and is painful

sprang see **spring**

sprawl to sit or lie with your arms and legs spread out

spray to make tiny drops of liquid fall all over something

spread 1 to stretch something out to its full size
The bird **spread** *its wings.*
2 to make something cover a surface

spring 1 the part of the year when plants start to grow and the days are getting lighter and warmer
2 a place where water comes out of the ground
3 a piece of metal wound into rings so that it jumps back into shape after it has been pressed or stretched
4 to move suddenly upward
I **sprang** *up and caught the ball. Weeds had* **sprung** *up everywhere.*

sprinkle to make a few tiny pieces or drops fall on something

sprint to run a short distance very quickly

sprout 1 to start to grow
The seeds soon **sprouted.**
2 small shoots that grow from a plant

sprung see **spring**

spun see **spin**

spurt 1 to move like water shooting suddenly upward

2 to move faster near the end of a race

spy 1 someone who works secretly to find out things about another person or country
2 to notice
I **spied** the bird right away.
3 to be a spy

squabble to quarrel about something that is not important

square 1 a flat shape with four straight sides that are all the same length
2 a public area in the centre of a town

squash 1 to press something hard so that it goes out of shape
2 a game played indoors with rackets and a small rubber ball

squat to sit on the ground with your knees bent

squeak to make the tiny, shrill sound a mouse makes

squeal to make a long, shrill sound

squeeze to press something between your hands or two other things

squid a sea creature with eight short arms and two very long ones

squirm to twist and turn the body about, like a worm

squirrel a small animal with a very thick tail that lives in trees

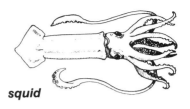

squid

squirt to make a thin stream of liquid come suddenly out of something

stab to hit someone with the sharp, pointed end of a knife or sword

stable a building in which horses are kept

stack a neat pile

stadium a large place where people can watch sports and games

staff 1 a group of people who work together in an office, store or school
2 a thick stick for walking with

stag a male deer

stage 1 a raised floor in a hall or theatre, on which people act, sing, or dance to entertain other people
2 the point someone has reached in doing something

stagger to try to stand or walk but find it difficult to stay upright

stagnant not flowing or fresh
a pool of **stagnant** water

stain a dirty mark made on something

stair one of a set of steps for going up or down inside a building

staircase a set of stairs and banisters

stake a thick, pointed stick

stale not fresh
stale bread

stalk 1 a thin stem
2 to walk in a stiff way that shows you are angry
3 to move secretly to get close to an animal you are hunting

stall 1 a kind of small shop or a table that things are sold on. Markets have stalls.
2 a place for one animal in a stable or shed

stallion a male horse

stammer to keep repeating the sounds at the beginning of words when you speak

stamp 1 to bang a foot heavily on the ground
2 a piece of sticky paper with a picture on it. People put stamps on letters to pay for delivery.

stand 1 to be on your feet without moving
I **stood** *there until they came.*
2 something made for putting things on
a cake **stand,** *a hat* **stand**

standard 1 how good something is
a high **standard** *of work*
2 a flag

stank see **stink**

star 1 one of the tiny, bright lights you see in the sky at night
2 a famous singer or actor

starch a powder or liquid for making clothes stiff

stare to look at someone or something for a long time, without moving your eyes

starling a dark brown bird often seen in large flocks

start 1 to take the first steps in doing something
2 to make something happen

startle to make a person or animal very surprised and frightened
startling **news**

starvation illness or death caused by great hunger

starve to be very ill or die because you have not had enough food

state 1 how someone or something is
2 to say something important
3 a country or part of a country

statement words that say something important

station 1 a place where people

get on or off trains
2 a building for police or firemen

statue a model of a person made in stone or metal

stay 1 to be in the same place
2 to live somewhere as a visitor

steady not shaking in any way
a **steady** voice, a **steady** hand

steak (rhymes with rake)
a thick slice of meat or fish

steal to take something that does not belong to you and keep it
A dog **stole** the meat yesterday. The jewels were **stolen.**

steam very hot water that has turned into a gas that cannot be seen

steel a strong, shiny metal made from iron

steep sloping sharply
a **steep** hill

steeple a tall, pointed tower on top of a church

steer 1 to make a ship, car, or bicycle go in the direction you want
2 a young bull kept for its meat

stem 1 the main part of a plant above the ground
2 the thin part that joins a leaf, flower, or fruit to the rest of the plant

step 1 the movement you make with your foot when you are walking, running, or dancing
2 a flat place where you can put your foot when you are going up or down something

stepfather a man who is married to your mother but is not your real father

stepmother a woman who is married to your father but is not your real mother

stern 1 the back end of a boat
2 severe or strict

stew 1 meat and vegetables cooked in liquid
2 to cook something slowly in liquid

stick 1 a long, thin piece of wood
2 a long, thin piece of anything
a **stick** of licorice
3 to become fastened or joined to things, as glue and mud do
The candy was **stuck** to the bag.
4 to press a sharp point into something

stickhandle to move a hockey puck back and forth with a hockey stick

sticky able to become fastened to other things. Glue, jam, and honey are all sticky.

stiff not easily bent
stiff cardboard

still 1 not moving
*Hold it **still.***
2 the same now as before
*He is **still** ill.*

stilts a pair of poles with which you can walk high above the ground

sting 1 a sharp part with poison on it that some animals and plants have
2 to hurt someone with a sting
*A bee **stung** me yesterday.*

stink to have a very strong, bad smell
*The stable was filthy and **stank.***

stir 1 to move a liquid or a soft mixture around with a spoon
2 to start to move

stirrup the metal part that hangs down each side of a horse's saddle for you to put your foot in while you are riding

stitch 1 a loop of thread made by the needle in sewing
2 one of the loops of wool on a knitting needle

3 a sudden pain in the side. People sometimes get stitches when they have been running.

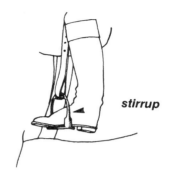

stirrup

stock a lot of things kept ready to be sold or used

stocking a covering for the foot and leg worn next to the skin

stoke to put coal or wood on a fire to keep it burning

stole, stolen see **steal**

stomach the part in the middle of the body, where food goes when it is eaten

stone 1 rock
2 a small piece of rock
3 the hard seed in the middle of a cherry, plum, peach, or apricot

stood see **stand**

stool a small seat without a back

stoop to bend the body forward

stop 1 to end

2 to come to rest
*The bus **stopped.***
3 to stay

store 1 to keep things until they are needed
2 a place where you can buy things

stork a large bird with very long legs and a long beak

storm a very strong wind with a lot of rain or snow

story 1 words that tell you about something that has really happened or about something that someone has made up
*adventure **stories***
2 one of the levels of a building

stout fat
*a **stout** lady*

stove something that gives out heat for warming a room or for cooking

straight 1 like a line drawn with a ruler
*a **straight** road*
2 straight away at once

straighten 1 to make something straight
2 to become straight

strain 1 to stretch, push, or try too hard
2 to hurt part of yourself by stretching or pushing too hard
3 to separate a liquid from

lumps or other things floating in it. People strain tea to get rid of the tea leaves.

strange 1 not known or seen before
*a **strange** place*
2 unusual and very surprising
*a **strange** story*

stranger 1 someone in a place he does not know
2 someone you do not know

strap a flat strip of leather or another strong material for fastening things together

straw 1 dry stalks of grain
2 a very thin tube for drinking through

strawberry a small, red, juicy fruit
***strawberry** jam*

stray lost and without a home
*a **stray** cat*

streak 1 a long, narrow mark
2 to move very quickly

stream water that is moving along in one direction

streamer a long strip of paper or a ribbon joined by one end to something to decorate it

street a road with buildings along each side

strength how strong someone or something is

stretch to pull something to

make it longer, wider, or tighter

stretcher a pair of poles with canvas stretched across them for carrying a sick or injured person

strict keen on always being obeyed

stride to walk with long steps
*I **strode** angrily out of the room.*

strike 1 to hit
*The house was **struck** by lightning.*
2 to strike a match to rub a match along something rough so that it bursts into flame
3 to stop working in order to get something from the people in charge

string very thin rope

strip 1 a long, narrow piece
2 to take off clothes or a covering

stripe a coloured band across or down something

strode see **stride**

stroke 1 to move the hand gently along something
2 a hitting movement

stroll to walk slowly, because you are enjoying your walk and do not have to get anywhere

strong 1 healthy and able to do things that need a lot of energy
*a **strong** horse*
2 not easily broken
***strong** rope*
3 with a lot of flavour
***strong** tea*

struck see **strike**

structure 1 anything that has been built
2 the way something has been built

struggle 1 to use your arms and legs in fighting or trying to get free
2 to try very hard to do something you find difficult

stubborn not willing to change your ideas even though they might be wrong

stuck see **stick**

student someone who studies at a school

studio a place where films or radio or television programs are made

study 1 to spend time learning about something
2 to look at something very carefully
3 a room where someone studies

stuff 1 anything used for making things
2 to fill something tightly
3 to push something inside another thing

stuffy without fresh air
a **stuffy** room

stumble to fall over something

stump the part of a broken tree, tooth, or pencil that is left

stun 1 to hit or hurt someone so much that he cannot think properly
2 to make someone very surprised

stung see **sting**

stunk see **stink**

stupid 1 very silly
a **stupid** idea
2 slow to learn and understand

sturdy strong and healthy
a **sturdy** child

stutter to keep repeating words and sounds when you speak

sty a sore swelling on the edge of a eyelid

style the way something is done or made

subject 1 the person or thing that you are writing about or learning about
2 someone who is ruled by a king, queen, or government

submarine a ship that can travel under water

substance anything that can be seen, touched, or used for making things

subtract to find the answer to a question like this 6-3 =

subway 1 a train that runs underground
2 a tunnel made under the ground so that people can get to the other side of a road safely

succeed to do or get what you wanted to do or get

successful able to do or get what you wanted to do or get

such 1 of the same kind
toys **such** as these
2 so great
It was **such** a surprise!

suck 1 to take in air or liquid from something
I **sucked** milk through a straw.
2 to keep moving something around inside your mouth without chewing it
He **sucked** a candy.

sudden happening quickly without any warning

*a **sudden** scream*

suede (swade)
a kind of soft leather that is not shiny

suet (soo-it)
a hard fat that comes from sheep and cattle

suffer to have to put up with pain or something else that is not pleasant

sufficient enough

sugar a sweet food that is put in other foods to make them taste sweet

suggest to give someone an idea that you think is useful

suit 1 a jacket and a pair of trousers or skirt that are meant to be worn together
2 to fit in with someone's plans
3 to look well on someone
*That colour **suits** you.*

suitable just right for something
suitable shoes for dancing

suitcase a kind of box with a lid and a handle, for carrying clothes and other things on journeys

suite (sweet)
a set of furniture

sulk to stop speaking to your friends, because you are angry about something

summer the hottest part of the year

summit the top of a mountain

sun the large, round light in the sky that gives the Earth heat and light

sundial a kind of clock that uses a shadow made by the sun to show what time it is

sung see **sing**

sunk see **sink**

sunny with sun shining
*a **sunny** day*

sunrise the time when the sun rises

sunset the time when the sun goes down

sunshine the light and heat that come from the sun when it is shining

supermarket a large store where people help themselves to items as they go around and pay for them all on the way out

supersonic faster than sound travels
*a **supersonic** airplane*

supper a meal or snack eaten in the evening

supply 1 to give what is needed **2** things kept ready to be used when needed
*a **supply** of paper*

support 1 to hold up something so that it does not fall **2** to give help to someone

suppose to think something is true although it might not be

sure knowing something is true or right
*I'm **sure** their house is blue.*

surface 1 the part all around the outside of something **2** the top of a table or desk

surgeon a doctor who is trained to do operations

surname your last name that is the same as your family's name

surprise 1 the feeling you have when something suddenly happens that you were not expecting **2** something that happens and was not expected

surrender to stop fighting and agree to obey the enemy

surround to be all around someone or something

suspect to have a feeling that there might be something wrong

suspicious feeling that there might be something wrong
*a **suspicious** policeman*

swallow 1 to make something go down your throat **2** a bird with a dark blue body, a long tail, and pointed wings

swam see **swim**

swamp an area of very wet ground

swan a big white bird with a very long neck that lives on water or near to it

swap (*rhymes with* hop) to change one thing for another thing

swarm a large number of insects together
*a **swarm** of bees*

sway to move from side to side

swear 1 to make a very serious promise
*He has **sworn** to tell the truth.* **2** to use bad words
*He **swore** when he hit his finger.*

sweat to lose liquid through your skin, because you are ill or very hot

sweep to use a brush to clear away dust and litter from

something
*I **swept** this floor yesterday.*

sweet 1 with the taste of sugar or honey
2 very pleasant

swell to get bigger
*My broken ankle has **swollen.***

swelling a swollen place on the body

swept see **sweep**

swerve to move suddenly to one side so that you will not bump into something

swift quick

swim 1 to move the body through water, without touching the bottom
*I **swam** a length yesterday.*
2 to cross water by swimming
*She has **swum** across the river.*

swindle to make someone believe something that is not true in order to get something valuable from him

swing 1 to move back and forth, from side to side, or in a curve
*The door **swung** open in the wind.*
2 a seat hung from a tree or metal bar so that it can move back and forth

swipe to hit hard

swirl to move around quickly in circles

switch 1 anything that is turned or pressed in order to make something work or stop working
*an electric light **switch***
2 to change from one thing to another

swollen see **swell**

swoop to fly down suddenly to attack something

sword (sord)
a weapon like a knife with a very long blade

swore, sworn see **swear**

swum see **swim**

swung see **swing**

syllable (silabul)
any word or part of a word that has one separate sound when you say it. Bi-cy-cle has three syllables and bike has one syllable.

symmetrical with two halves that are exactly alike but the opposite way around. Butterflies and wheels are symmetrical.

sympathy the feeling you have when you are sorry for someone who is sad, ill, or in trouble, and want to help him

synthetic manufactured rather than natural
*Plastic is a **synthetic** material.*

syrup a very sweet, sticky liquid

system a set of parts, things, or ideas that work together

Tt

tabby 1 a gray or brown cat with dark stripes in its fur
2 a female cat

table 1 a piece of furniture with a flat top and legs
2 a list of facts arranged in order

tablecloth a piece of material spread over a table to cover it

tablespoon a spoon for serving food

tablet a small, solid piece of medicine

tack a short nail with a flat top

tackle 1 to try to do a job that needs doing
2 to try to knock over someone who is carrying the ball in a football game
3 all the things needed for doing something
*fishing **tackle***

tadpole a tiny creature that lives in water and will turn into a frog

or toad when it grows up

tag 1 a piece of thin cardboard or other material on which is written the price of an item
*This price **tag** says four dollars.*
2 a game in which one person who is "it" must chase and touch another person and make her "it"
3 to follow
*Our dog always **tags** along when we ride our bikes.*
4 to put a tag on
***Tag** those chairs with 'For Sale' notices.*

tail the part at the end of something. Most animals have tails and so do airplanes.

tailor someone whose job is to make clothes

take 1 to get hold of something
*He **took** his prize and smiled.*
2 to carry or lead away
*The money was **taken** yesterday.*
*Dad is **taking** us to the zoo.*

tale a story

talent the ability to something very well
*a **talent** for singing*

talk to speak to other people

talkative fond of talking

tall measuring more than usual from top to bottom
*a **tall** person, a **tall** tree*

tambourine a musical instrument that you shake or hit with your fingers

tame not wild or dangerous. Tame animals can be kept as pets, because they are not frightened of people.

tamper to make changes in something so that it will not work properly
*I **tampered** with the car so that it would not start.*

tan 1 skin that has gone brown because of the sun
2 light brown
3 to make the skin of an animal into leather

tangerine a kind of small orange

tangled twisted up in knots
***tangled** wool, **tangled** hair*

tank 1 a large container for liquid. Fish tanks are made of glass and hot water tanks are made of metal.
2 a kind of very strong, heavy car used in war. It has a big gun on top and two long strips of metal around its wheels so that it can move over rough ground.

tanker 1 a large ship for carrying oil

2 a truck for carrying liquids

tap 1 see **faucet**
2 a light touch or knock
3 to drill a hole into something to get something else out of it
*Did you **tap** your maple trees yet?*

tape 1 a narrow strip of cotton used in tying things and making loops or labels for clothes
2 a narrow strip of special plastic used in a tape-recorder

taper 1 a kind of very thin candle used for lighting fires
2 to become very narrow at one end

tape measure a ruler made out of cloth tape or thin metal

tape recorder a machine that can take sound down on special tape or make sound come out of a tape

tapestry a piece of strong cloth covered with stitches that make a picture

tar a thick, black, sticky liquid made from coal or wood and used for making roads or for roofs

199

tardy lagging behind, late
*Marika is always on time and her brother is always **tardy.***

target something that people aim at and try to hit

tart 1 pastry with jam or fruit on it **2** very sour. Rhubarb without sugar tastes tart.

tartan Scottish woollen cloth woven with a check pattern and used for making kilts and other items of clothing

task a piece of work that must be done

tassel a bundle of threads tied together at the top and used to decorate things

taste 1 to eat a little bit of food or sip a drink to see what it is like **2** the flavour something has when you taste it

tasty with a strong, pleasant taste
tasty pizza

tattered badly torn

taught see **teach**

tax money that people have to give to the government

taxi a car that you can travel in if you pay the driver
*two **taxis***

tea 1 a hot drink made with boiling water and the dried leaves of a tea-plant **2** a meal eaten in the afternoon

teach to make someone else able to understand or do something
*She **taught** me to swim last year.*

teacher someone whose job is to teach

team a group of people who work together or play together on the same side in a game

teapot a kind of jug with a spout and lid, used for making tea

tear[1] (*rhymes with* fear) a small drop of water that comes out of the eye when you cry

tear[2] (*rhymes with* fair) to pull something apart so that you damage it
*I **tore** the letter up and threw it away.*
*His coat was **torn.***

tease to bother or annoy someone for fun
*Stop **teasing** her!*

teaspoon a small spoon used to eat food or to stir coffee and tea

teem 1 to rain very hard **2** to be full of moving things
*The river was **teeming** with fish.*

teenager someone who is between thirteen and nineteen years old

teeth more than one tooth

telegram a short message sent very quickly along electric wires

telegraph to send a telegram

telephone 1 an instrument that makes sound travel along wires so that you can speak to someone far away
2 to use a telephone to speak to someone

telephone pole a tall pole that holds up telephone wires

telescope a tube with lenses at each end. People look through telescopes in order to see things that are far away.

television a machine that receives pictures and sound through the air so that people can watch them

tell to speak in order to pass on news, a story, or instructions
I **told** you about it yesterday.

temper 1 the mood someone is in

in a good **temper**
in a bad **temper**
2 to lose your temper to become very angry

temperature how hot or cold something is

temple a place where some people worship

temporary for a short time only

tempt to try to make someone do wrong

temptation something that makes you want to do wrong

tend 1 to be likely to do something
He **tends** to fall asleep after dinner.
2 to look after

tender 1 loving
a **tender** smile
2 soft
tender meat
3 sore
tender skin

tennis a game played by two or four people with rackets and a ball on a court with a net across the middle

tent a kind of shelter made of canvas stretched over poles. People sleep in tents when they are camping.

tepee a kind of tent in a cone shape once used by Indians of North America

tepee

term a length of time
*The school **term** this year is 199 days.*

terminal 1 the place where a bus, train, or airplane stops to let people off or on
2 the part of a computer that you work with

terrace 1 a raised, flat piece of ground next to a house or in a garden
2 a row of houses that are joined together

terrapin a creature that lives in water and looks like a small tortoise

terrible very bad
terrible weather

terrier a kind of small dog

terrific 1 very good
*a **terrific** idea*
2 very big
*a **terrific** bang*

terrify to make a person or animal very frightened

territory land that belongs to one country or person

terror great fear

test 1 questions you have to answer to show how good you are at something
*a spelling **test***
2 to try out
***Test** the brakes.*

tether to tie an animal so that it has room to move about, but cannot get away

than compared with another person or thing
*You are smaller **than** I.*

thank to tell someone you are pleased about something he has given you or done for you
***Thank** you for the present.*

thankful wanting to thank someone for what he has done
*She felt very **thankful**.*

that the one there
***That** is mine, this is yours.*
***Those** books are yours.*

thaw 1 to make ice or snow melt
2 the melting of ice or snow

the a word used to mean a certain person or animal or thing
***The** book I want is not here.*

theatre, theater a place where people go to see plays, shows, and movies

theft stealing
*the **theft** of the diamond*

their belonging to them
***their** coats*

them see **they**

themselves 1 they and no one else
2 by themselves on their own

theme the main idea of a subject, story, or project

then 1 after that
2 at that time
*We didn't know about it **then**.*

there in that place or to that place
*Stand **there**!*

therefore and so

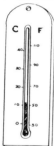

thermometer an instrument that measures temperature

these see **this**

they the people or things you are talking about
***They** all like cake.*
*I gave each of **them** a treat.*

thick measuring a lot from one side to the other
*a **thick** slice of cake*

thicken 1 to make thicker
2 to get thicker

thief someone who steals things
*Ali Baba and the forty **thieves***

thigh the top part of the leg down to the knee

thimble a metal or plastic cover for the end of a finger. You wear it when you sew to protect your finger from the needle.

thin not fat or thick

thing anything that can be seen or touched

think 1 to use your mind
2 to have an idea
*I **thought** you were wrong.*

third 1 one of the three equal parts something can be divided into. It can also be written as ⅓.
2 coming after the second
***third** prize*

thirst the need for drink

thirsty wanting a drink

this the one here
***This** is mine, that is yours.*
***These** books are mine.*

thistle a wild plant with prickly leaves and purple flowers

thong 1 a thin piece of leather like a shoe lace

2 a shoe like a sandal with only a strap on the upper part to keep the shoe on the foot

thorn a sharp, pointed part on a plant's stem. Roses have thorns.

thorough 1 done properly and carefully
thorough work
2 complete
a *thorough* mess

those see **that**

though and yet or although
*It was very cold **though** it didn't snow.*

thought 1 see **think**
2 something that you think

thoughtful 1 thinking a lot
*She looked **thoughtful**.*
2 thinking kindly about others and what they would like

thread 1 a long, thin piece of cotton, nylon, or wool used for sewing or weaving cloth
2 to put thread through the eye of a needle or the hole in a bead

threat a promise that you will do something bad if what you want does not happen

threaten to make threats

thresh to get the seeds out of grain

threw see **throw**

thrill a sudden excited feeling

thrilling very exciting

throat the front of the neck and the tube inside it that takes food, liquid, and air into the body

throb to beat heavily. Your heart throbs when you have been running very fast.

throne a special chair for a king or queen

throng a large number of people

throttle the lever on a tractor or other machine that you use to make it run slower or faster

through from one end or side to the other
*We went **through** the tunnel.*

throughout all through
*It was hot **throughout** the day.*

throw to make something move through the air
*He **threw** a stone over the barn roof.*
*The rock was **thrown** into the sea.*

thrust to push hard
*He **thrust** his sword into the ground.*

thud to make the low, dull sound something heavy and large makes when it hits the ground

thumb the short, thick finger at the side of each hand

thump to hit hard with the fist

thunder the loud noise that you hear after a flash of lightning in a storm

thunderstorms a storm with thunder and lightning

tick 1 to make the sound a clock or watch keeps making when it is working
2 a small mark like this √

ticket a piece of paper or card that you buy so that you can travel on a bus or train or get into places like theatres

tickle to keep touching part of someone's body lightly with your fingers or a feather. Most people laugh when they are tickled.

tide the movement of the sea toward the land and away from the land

tidy neatly arranged with nothing out of place
a **tidy** room

tie 1 to fasten something with a knot or bow
He's **tying** a ribbon around the parcel.
2 see **necktie**

tiger a big wild cat found in India

and China. It has yellow fur with black stripes.

tight fitting very closely
tight shoes, a **tight** lid

tighten 1 to make tighter
2 to get tighter

tile 1 a hard clay tube like a pipe that is used to drain away water under ground
2 a hard, flat square piece of material used to cover the floor in buildings

till 1 until
2 a drawer or box for money in a store

tilt to make something slope

timber wood that can be used for making things

time 1 seconds, minutes, hours, days, weeks, months, and years
2 a certain moment in the day
What **time** is it? It's **time** for recess.
3 the rhythm and speed of a piece of music

timetable a list that shows when something is supposed to happen
Look at the **timetable** to see when the train leaves for Thunder Bay.

timid not brave

tingle to sting a little bit
Her ears were **tingling** with the cold.

tinkle to make the light, ringing sound a small bell makes

tinsel thin, shiny, silver ribbon. Tinsel is used for decorating things at Christmas

tiny very small

tip 1 the part right at the end of something
2 a small gift of money given to someone for his help
3 to turn something over so that the things inside fall out

tire a circle of rubber around the rim of a wheel

tiptoe to walk on your toes without making a sound
She **tiptoed** away.

tired 1 needing to rest or sleep
2 bored with something
I'm **tired** of work.

tissue very thin, soft paper

title 1 the name of a book, film, picture, or piece of music
2 a word like Sir, Lady, Dr, Mr, and Ms that is put in front of a person's name

titter to laugh in a silly way

to 1 in the direction of
Move **to** the side please.
2 for
Is this the top **to** the bottle?
3 against
Move the chair over **to** the wall.

4 until
Recess lasted from 10:00 a.m. **to** 10:30 a.m.
5 along with
We danced **to** the music.
6 before
The time is now five minutes **to** five.
7 as far as
Come with me **to** the corner.
8 rather than
I prefer reading **to** singing.

toad an animal like a big frog. It has rough, dry skin and lives on land

toadstool a plant that looks like a mushroom

toast bread cooked until it is crisp and brown

tobacco a plant with leaves that are dried and smoked in pipes or used to make cigars and cigarettes

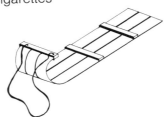

toboggan a kind of sleigh used for sliding down slopes covered in snow

today this day

toddler a young child just beginning to walk

toe one of the five separate parts at the end of each foot

toffee butter and sugar cooked together

together 1 with another
joined together
2 at the same time as another
They sang together

toil to do hard work

toilet a large bowl with a seat. Toilets are used to get rid of waste from the body.

token a round piece of plastic or a kind of ticket, used instead of money to pay for something
bus tokens

told see **tell**

tomato a soft, round, red vegetable with seeds inside it

tomb (*rhymes with* room) a place where a dead person's body is buried. Some tombs are above the ground.

tomorrow the day after today

tone 1 a musical sound
2 the kind of sound someone's voice has
a gentle tone

tongs a tool that looks like a pair of scissors and is used for getting hold of something and picking it up

tongue the long, soft, pink part that moves about inside the mouth

tonight this evening or night

tonne a unit of measure
a tonne of corn

tonsils parts of the throat that sometimes cause an illness called tonsillitis

too 1 as well
Can I come too?
2 more than is needed
too much

took see **take**

tool something that you use to help you to do a job. Hammers and saws are tools.

tooth one of the hard, white parts in the mouth
Brush your teeth after every meal

toothache a pain in a tooth

toothbrush a small brush with a long handle, for cleaning teeth

toothpaste a thick paste put on a toothbrush and used for cleaning teeth

top 1 the upper limit of something
The top of the hill.
2 the upper surface of something

*The **top** of the table.*
3 a toy that is spun on a pointed end

topic something interesting that you are writing about or talking about

topple to fall over because there is too much on top
*The pile of bricks **toppled** over.*

topsoil the surface layer of soil

tore see **tear**²

torment to keep bothering or annoying someone for fun, although it is cruel

torn see **tear**²

torpedo a kind of long, round bomb sent under water to destroy ships and submarines
*two **torpedoes***

torrent a very fast stream of water

tortoise a creature with four legs and a shell over its body, that moves slowly

torture 1 great pain that seems as if it will never end
2 to make someone feel great pain

toss to throw into the air

total the amount when you have added everything up

totem pole a tall pole like a telephone pole with faces and figures carved into it and painted. Totem poles were first made by Indian people on the west coast of Canada.

totter to walk very shakily as if you are going to fall over. Young children totter when they are learning to walk.

touch 1 to feel something with part of your body
*He **touched** the wet paint with his finger.*
2 to be so close to something else that there is no space in between

tough 1 strong
***tough** shoes, a **tough** fighter*
2 hard to chew
***tough** meat*

tour 1 a journey you make to visit different places
2 to walk around a place looking at different things

tow to pull along with a rope or chain
*The truck **towed** the car to a garage.*

toward, towards in the direction of something
*He walked **toward** the school.*

towel a piece of cloth for drying things that are wet
*a bath **towel**, a tea **towel***

tower 1 a tall, narrow building
*the C.N. **tower***
2 a tall, narrow part of a building
*a church **tower***

town a place with schools, stores, offices, factories, and a lot of houses built near each other

township an area of a province set aside for local government
*A county has several **townships** in it.*

toy something you play with

trace 1 a mark left by something
2 to copy a picture using thin paper that you can see through. You put the paper over the picture and follow its lines with a pencil.

track 1 a kind of path
2 a railway line
3 to follow the marks left by a person or animal

tractor a machine with wheels and an engine that is used on farms to pull heavy things

trade buying and selling

tradition a custom that people are used to doing. Very often people have forgotten when or how a tradition started.
*Giving gifts at Christmas is a **tradition.***

traffic cars, buses, bicycles, trucks, and other things travelling on the road

traffic light a set of coloured lights that tells cars and pedestrians to stop or go

tragedy 1 something very sad that has happened
2 a play with a very sad ending

trail 1 a rough path
2 smells and marks left behind by an animal. People follow trails when they are hunting.
3 to be dragged along the ground
*Your scarf is **trailing** in the mud.*

trailer something that is pulled along by a car or truck

train 1 railway cars joined together and pulled by an engine
2 to teach a person or animal how to do something
3 to practise for a competition or game

traitor someone who gives away a secret or gives information about his friends or country to the enemy

tramp 1 someone without a home or job who walks from place to place

2 to walk heavily

trample to spoil something by walking heavily on it

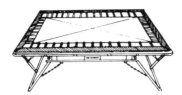

trampoline a large piece of canvas joined to a metal frame with springs for bouncing up and down on

trance a kind of sleep

transfer to move someone or something to another place *He was **transferred** to a different team.*

transistor radio a kind of radio that you can carry about with you easily

transparent so clear that you can see through it. Glass is transparent.

transport to take people, animals, or things from one place to another

trap 1 something made for catching an animal and keeping it prisoner
2 to catch a person or animal by using a trap or a clever trick

trapdoor a kind of door in the floor or ceiling

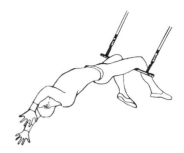

trapeze a bar hanging from ropes, used by acrobats

travel to go from one place to another

trawler a fishing boat that pulls a large net along in the water

tray a flat piece of wood or tin used for carrying food, cups, plates, and other light things

treacherous not to be trusted *The **treacherous** guard killed the king.*

treason giving away your country's secrets to the enemy

treasure gold, silver, jewels, or other valuable things

treat 1 to behave toward someone or something in a certain way
*The horse had been badly **treated.***
2 to pay for another person's food or drink
3 something special that pleases you very much
*a birthday **treat***

tree any tall plant with leaves, branches, and a thick stem of wood

tremble to shake because you are cold or frightened

tremendous very large or great
a **tremendous** explosion

trench a long, narrow hole dug in the ground

trespass to go on someone else's land, without asking her if you can

trial 1 trying something out to see how well it works
2 the time when a prisoner is in court. The people there decide whether or not she has done something wrong.

triangle a flat shape with three straight edges and three corners

tribe a group of families who live together and are ruled by one leader

trick 1 something very clever that a person or animal has learned to do
2 to make someone believe something that is not true

trickle to move like a very small stream of water

tricky something that is very difficult to do

tricycle a machine with three wheels and two pedals that is ridden

tried see **try**

trifle 1 cake and fruit covered in jelly, custard, and cream
2 something unimportant
He is always bothering about **trifles.**
3 just a little
The salad is a **trifle** sour.

trigger the part of a gun that is pulled to fire it

trim 1 to cut away the parts of something to make it neat and tidy
2 to decorate a piece of clothing
a coat **trimmed** with fur

trio a set of three people or things

trip 1 a short journey
a school **trip**
2 to fall over something
I **tripped** over the log and broke my leg.

triumphant very pleased because you have been successful
a **triumphant** smile

trod, trodden see **tread**

troll 1 a small dwarf that is usually quite unpleasant in his manner
2 to try to catch fish by hanging hooks and lines from a moving boat

trolley a small, narrow table on wheels

troop an organized group of people

tropical belonging to the very hot countries in Africa, Asia, and South America
tropical plants

trot one of the ways a horse can move. It is faster than a walk but slower than a gallop.

trouble 1 something that upsets, worries, or bothers you
2 to take trouble over something to take great care when you are doing something

trough (troff)
a long, narrow container that holds food or water for farm animals
*a pig **trough**, a horse **trough***

trousers a piece of clothing that covers the body from the waist to the ankles and has separate parts for the legs
*a pair of **trousers***

trout a fish found in rivers and lakes

trowel

trowel a small spade with a short handle

truant a pupil who stays away from school without permission

truck a vehicle with a motor and seats like a car but with a large box on the back for hauling things

trudge to walk slowly and heavily because you are tired

true correct or real
*a **true** story, a **true** friend*

truly in a true or honest way

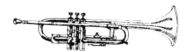

trumpet a brass musical instrument that is blown

trunk 1 a tree's thick stem
2 an elephant's long nose
3 a large box with a lid and handle for carrying things on a journey or storing things

trust to believe that someone or something will not let you down

truth something that is true

try 1 to work at something you want to be able to do
2 to test something
*I **tried** it out before I bought it.*

tub a round container
*a **tub** of ice cream*

tube 1 a long, thin, round container
*a **tube** of toothpaste*
2 a long, thin, hollow piece of plastic, rubber, glass, or metal. Tubes are used for taking water and gas from one place to another.

tuck to tidy away the loose ends of something
*She **tucked** her blouse into her skirt.*

tuft a number of feathers, hairs, or blades of grass growing together

tug 1 to pull hard
2 a boat used for pulling ships

tulip a spring flower that grows from a bulb and is shaped like a cup

tumble to fall

tumbler a glass with a flat bottom
*a **tumbler** of water*

tuna a very large ocean fish that is good to eat

tune a series of notes that make a piece of music

tunic 1 a short dress worn over a skirt or trousers
2 a kind of long jacket worn as part of a uniform

tunnel a long hole that has been made under the ground or through a hill

turban a covering for the head made by wrapping cloth around it in a special way

turbine a kind of engine with a wheel inside it turned by gas, water, or steam

turf short grass and the soil it is growing in

turkey a large bird kept for its meat

turn 1 to move around
2 to change
*The Prince **turned** into a frog.*
3 to become
*She **turned** pale.*
4 a time for you to do something that others have done or are still waiting to do
*It's his **turn** to set the table.*

turnip a round, white vegetable

turntable the part of a record-player that you put the record on

turpentine a kind of oil that can be used for cleaning paint brushes and mixed with paint to make it thinner

turret a small tower in a castle

turtle a sea creature that looks like a tortoise

tusk one of two long, pointed teeth such as an elephant has

tweed warm cloth woven from wool
a **tweed** coat

tweezers a small tool for getting hold of very thin things such as stamps
a pair of **tweezers**

twice two times

twig a small, thin branch

twilight the dim light at the end of the day before it gets completely dark

twin one of two children born to the same mother at the same time

twine thin, strong string

twinkle to shine with a lot of tiny flashes of bright light. Stars twinkle.

twirl to turn around and around quickly

twist 1 to turn or bend
a **twisted** ankle
2 to wrap things around each other

twitch to keep making quick movements with part of the body. Rabbits twitch their noses.

twitter to keep making quick, light sounds like a bird

type 1 one kind or sort
2 to write with a typewriter

typewriter a machine with keys that you press in order to print letters and numbers

ugly not pleasant to look at

umbrella a round piece of cloth stretched over a frame that can be opened and shut. You hold an umbrella over your head to keep off the rain.

umpire someone who makes sure that the rules are kept in games such as baseball and tennis

uncle your aunt's husband or the brother of one of your parents

uncomfortable not comfortable

unconscious (un-kon-shuss) in a very deep sleep

After the accident he was **unconscious** *for a week.*

under below

underground under the ground

undergrowth bushes and other plants growing under tall trees

underline to draw a straight line underneath a word

underneath in a place under something

understand to know what something means or how it works
*He **understood** what the stranger said.*

undertow a flow of water that moves in a different direction from the water on the surface
*An **undertow** can be very dangerous for swimmers.*

underwear clothes made to be worn under other clothes

undo to open something that has been fastened
*I **undid** the knot and opened the parcel.*
*Your shoe is **undone**.*

undress to take off clothes

uneven bumpy, not smooth or level

unfair not right or just

unfortunate not lucky

ungrateful not appreciating things that you have or that are done for you

unhappy sad, having no good feelings

unhealthy 1 ill, or always in danger of being ill
2 not good for you
*Too much sugar is **unhealthy** for you.*

unicorn a make-believe animal. It is like a horse, but has a long, straight horn growing out of the front of its head.

uniform the special clothes that

everyone in a group wears
*a school **uniform***
*a policeman's **uniform***

union a group of workers or other people who have joined together for an idea they all believe in

unique very unusual because it is the only one of its kind
*a **unique** painting*

unit an amount used in measuring or counting. Centimetres are units of length and dollars are units of money.

unite to join together to make one

universal having to do with everyone and everything

universe all the worlds that there are and everyone and everything in them

university a place where some people go to study when they have finished high school

unkind somewhat cruel, not kind

unless if not

unlike not like, different

unload 1 to take off the things that an animal, boat, car, or truck is carrying
*They **unloaded** the ship at the dock.*

2 to take the bullets out of a gun

unlock to open a door or box with a key

unnecessary not needed

unpleasant not attractive or enjoyable

unruly badly behaved and difficult to control

untidy messy

until up to a certain time
*I stayed up **until** midnight.*

unusual not occurring very often

unwell ill

unwrap to take something out of the paper it is wrapped in

up 1 to a higher place
*We walked **up** the hill.*
2 to a place farther along
*You will find it **up** the aisle.*
3 over, at an end
*The time for waiting is **up**.*
4 out of the ground
*Please pull **up** those weeds.*
5 out of bed
*I got **up** at dawn today.*
6 apart
*The dog tore **up** our newspaper.*
7 completely
*The hot sun has burned **up** our lawn.*

8 at bat
*Herbie is **up** after you.*

upon on or on top of

upper higher
*the **upper** lip*

upright 1 standing straight up
*an **upright** post*
2 honest
*an **upright person***

uproar loud noise made by people who are angry or excited about something

upset 1 to make someone unhappy
2 to knock over
*I **upset** the can and spilled the paint.*

upside-down turned over so that the bottom is at the top

upstairs the part of a house that you reach by climbing the stairs

upward, upwards moving to somewhere higher

urban having to do with the city
*Traffic is an **urban** problem.*

urge 1 to try to make someone hurry to do something
2 a sudden, strong wish to do something

urgent so important that it needs to be answered or done at once

*an **urgent** message*
urgent work

us a word used to refer to the person speaking or writing, as well as others who are there
*Lou came to see **us** last week.*

use to do a job with something
*I **used** paper and glue to make it.*

useful 1 able to be used a lot
*a **useful** tool*
2 helpful
***useful** information*

useless not useful

usual happening most often
*Dinner is at the **usual** time.*

utensil any tool, pot, or pan used in the kitchen

Vv

vacant with nobody in it
*a **vacant** room*

vaccination (vak-si-nation) an injection that keeps you from getting an illness

vacuum cleaner a machine that sucks up dust and dirt from floors and carpets

vague not clear or certain
a **vague** idea

vain 1 too proud of yourself and how you look
2 in vain without success
They tried **in vain** to move the log.

valley low land between hills

valuable worth a lot of money
valuable jewellery

value 1 the amount of money something could be sold for
2 how important or useful something is

valve a part in a machine that makes air, liquid, or electricity go in only one direction

van a kind of truck

vanilla flavouring that is used in desserts

vanish to go away suddenly and not be seen any more

vanity being too proud of yourself

vapour, vapor steam, mist, or smoke

variety 1 a lot of different kinds of things
a **variety** of flavours
2 a certain sort

various different, several

varnish a clear liquid painted on to wood or metal to make it shiny

vary to be different
varied designs

vase a jar for holding flowers

vast very large

veal meat from a calf

vegetable part of a plant used as food. Vegetables are usually eaten with the main part of a meal.

vehicle anything that takes people or things from one place to another on land. Cars, vans, buses, bicycles, trains, carts, and trucks are all vehicles.

veil a piece of thin material used to cover the face or head

vein one of the narrow tubes inside the body, that carry blood

velvet thick material that is smooth and soft on one side
a **velvet** dress

venom the poison of snakes

ventilator a kind of opening in a building for letting in fresh air

veranda a long, open place with a roof built on to the side of a house

verb any of the words that tell you what someone or something is doing. Come, go, sit, eat, sleep, and think are all verbs.

verse part of a poem or song

version a story about something that has happened
*His **version** of the accident is different from mine.*

vertical upright

very most
*Ice is **very** cold.*

vessel 1 any container for liquid **2** a boat or ship

vest a piece of clothing without sleeves worn on the top half of the body

vet someone whose job is to help animals that are ill or hurt. *Short for* veterinarian

vex to make someone angry

viaduct a long bridge that is a row of arches with a railway or road along the top of it

vicious (vish-uss)
bad and cruel

*a **vicious** kick, a **vicious** temper*

victim someone who has been hurt, robbed, or killed

victory the winning of a struggle or game

video game an electronic game in which the players move controls and watch the results on a television screen

view 1 everything that can be seen from one place **2** what a person thinks about something

vigour, vigor strength and energy

vile very nasty
*a **vile** smell*

village a group of houses and other buildings, in the country

villain a bad person

vine a plant that bunches of grapes grow on

vinegar a sour liquid put on food to make it taste better

violent very strong and rough
*a **violent** storm*

violet 1 a tiny purple or white flower that grows in spring **2** purple

violin a musical instrument made of wood with strings across it that are played with a bow

violin

visibility how clearly something can be seen. In fog visibility is poor.

visible able to be seen

vision 1 the ability to see
2 a kind of dream

visitor someone who goes to see a person or place

vivid 1 bright
vivid colours
2 lively
a *vivid* imagination
3 so clear it seems real
a *vivid* dream

vixen a female fox

vocabulary a list of the words someone uses

voice the sound you make with your mouth when you are speaking or singing

volcano a mountain that contains hot liquid, gases, and ash that sometimes burst out of it
two *volcanoes*

volley several things shot or thrown at the same time
a *volley* of bullets

volley ball a game with two teams on either side of a net. They hit a ball filled with air, back and forth across the net using their hands.

volume 1 the amount of space filled by something
2 one of a set of books
3 how loud a sound is

volunteer someone who offers to do something that she does not have to do

vote to say which person or idea you think should be chosen. Sometimes people vote by putting up their hands and sometimes by making a mark on a piece of paper.

voucher a printed paper you can use instead of money for buying certain things
a gift *voucher*

vow to make a serious promise

vowel any one of the letters a, e, i, o, u, and sometimes y

voyage a long journey by boat

voyageur an adventurous woodsman in early Canada who worked for a fur company carrying furs and supplies along the rivers

vulture a large bird that eats dead animals

Ww

wade to walk through water

wag to move quickly from side to side
*The dog **wagged** its tail.*

wage, wages the money paid to someone for the job he does

wagon a cart with four wheels

wail to make a long, sad cry

waist the narrow part in the middle of the body

wait to stay for something that you are expecting to happen

waiter a man who brings food to people in cafes, hotels, and restaurants

waitress a woman who brings food to people in cafes, hotels, and restaurants

wake to stop sleeping
***Wake** up!*
*He **woke** suddenly and saw the dog.*

walk to move along on foot

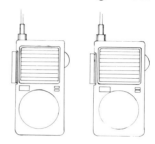

walkie-talkie a kind of radio that is carried about and can be used like a telephone

wall 1 a barrier made of bricks or stone put around a garden or field
2 one of the sides of a building or room

wallet a small, flat, leather case for money and papers that is carried in the pocket

walnut a kind of nut with a hard shell

walrus an animal like a seal but much larger and with tusks. Walruses live along the seashore in the far north.

waltz a kind of dance done with a partner

wampum a network of beads on a belt. Long ago wampum was used as money by some Indian tribes in North America.

wand a thin stick used for casting magic spells. In stories fairies and wizards have wands.

wander to move about without trying to get anywhere

want 1 to feel that you would like to have something **2** to need

war a fight between countries

ward a bedroom for patients in a hospital

wardrobe a cupboard where clothes are hung

warehouse a large building in which things are stored

wares things that are on sale

warm fairly hot
a **warm** room

warn to tell someone that he is in danger

warrior someone fighting in a battle

wart a dry, hard spot on the skin

was see **be**

wash to make something clean with water

washer 1 see **washing-machine** **2** a round flat piece of metal with a hole in it

washing clothes that need washing or are being washed

washing-machine a machine that washes clothes

wasp an insect that flies and can sting

waste 1 to use more of something than you need to **2** things that you get rid of because you do not need them any more.
waste paper

watch 1 to look at **2** a small clock that is worn or carried

watchperson someone whose job is to guard a building at night

water the clear liquid in rivers and seas. It falls from the sky as rain.

waterfall a stream of water falling from a high place to a low place

water lily a water plant that has large flowers at the surface of the water

watermelon a large green fruit oblong in shape. It is sweet, juicy, and red inside.

waterproof made of material that does not let water through
a **waterproof** coat

water ski one of a pair of short wide skis on which someone can ride on the top of the water if towed by a boat

watertight made so that water cannot get into it
watertight boots

wave 1 one of the lines of water you can see moving on the surface of the sea

2 to move your hand to say hello or goodbye to someone
3 the signals that come through the air to an antenna

wavy with curves in it
wavy hair, a **wavy** line

wax something that melts very easily and is used for making candles, crayons, and polish. Some wax is made by bees and some is made from oil.

way 1 a road or path
2 how something is done

we a word used to refer to the speaker or writer and other people
Jeff and I are leaving. **We** are going home.

weak not strong
a **weak** person, **weak** tea

weaken 1 to get weaker
2 to make weaker

wealth a lot of money or treasure

wealthy rich

weapon something used to hurt another person in a fight

wear 1 to be dressed in something
I **wore** that dress last time.
2 to wear out to become weak and useless because it has been used so much
3 to wear someone out to make someone very tired

223

*He was **worn** out after the game.*

weary very tired

weasel a small, furry animal with a long body. It eats mice, rats, and rabbits.

weather rain, snow, ice, fog, wind, and sun

weave to make material by pushing a thread under and over other threads
*She made a loom and **wove** a scarf on it.*
*The bag was **woven** in straw.*

web a thin, sticky net spun by a spider to trap insects

webfoot a foot with its toes joined together by skin. Ducks, otters, and other animals that swim a lot have webfeet.

wedding the time when a man and woman get married

wedge 1 a piece that is thick at one end and thin at the other like a triangle or the letter V
*a **wedge** of pie*
2 to keep two things apart by pushing something between them

weed any wild plant that grows where it is not wanted

week the seven days from Sunday to the next Saturday

weekend Saturday and Sunday

weep to let tears fall from the eyes
*He **wept** because he was lost.*

weigh 1 to find the weight of something
2 to have a certain weight

weight how heavy something is

weird (*rhymes with* beard) very strange

welcome to show that you are pleased when someone or something arrives

welfare 1 the health and happiness of people
2 money given by the government to people in need

well 1 healthy
2 in a good way
*He swims **well**.*
3 a hole dug to get water or oil out of the ground

went see **go**

wept see **weep**

were see **be**

west in the direction of the setting sun

western 1 from the west or in the west
2 a cowboy movie

wet covered with water or moisture

whack to hit hard with a stick

whale the largest sea animal there is

wharf a place where ships are loaded and unloaded

what 1 which thing
What is that?
2 that which
*Tell me **what** you think.*

whatever no matter what
***Whatever** happens, I'll help you.*

wheat a plant grown by farmers. Its seed is used for making flour.

wheel a circle of wood or metal fixed in the middle so that it can keep turning around. Cars, bicycles, carts, and some machines have wheels.

wheelbarrow a small cart with one wheel at the front, that is pushed

when 1 at what time
***When** are you coming?*
2 at the time that
***When** I moved, it flew away.*

whenever at any time

where in what place
***Where** are you?*

wherever no matter where
***Wherever** you are, I'll find you.*

whether if
*She asked **whether** I could come.*

which what person or thing
***Which** do you want?*

while in the time that something else is happening
*He fell asleep **while** the television was on.*

whimper the soft sound an animal or person makes when they are frightened or hurt

whine the long, sad sound an animal or person makes when they are unhappy

whip 1 a long piece of rope or leather joined to a handle and used for hitting things
2 to stir cream hard to make it thick
***whipped** cream*

whirl to turn around and around very quickly

whisk 1 to move very quickly
2 to stir hard

whisker a strong hair that grows on the faces of men and animals. A cat has long whiskers growing at each side of its mouth.

whisky a very strong drink

whisper to speak very softly

whistle 1 to make a shrill sound by blowing through the lips
2 something that makes a shrill sound when it is blown

who what person
Who did that?

whoever no matter what person
Whoever did it will be in trouble.

whole 1 not broken
*Swallow it **whole**.*
2 all or something
*the **whole** world*

whooping cough (hooping koff)
an illness that makes you keep coughing and breathing in heavily

whose belonging to what person
Whose is this?

why because of what
Why did you do that?

wick the string that goes through the middle of a candle

wicked very bad
*a **wicked** witch*

wide 1 measuring a lot from one side to the other
2 completely
wide awake, wide open

widow a woman whose husband has died

widower a man whose wife has died

width how wide something is

wiener a long, thin sausage

wife a woman married to someone
*Henry VIII had six **wives**.*

wig a covering of false hair worn on the head

wigwam a kind of tent used by certain North American Indian tribes long ago

wild 1 not looked after by people
*a **wild** flower*
2 not controlled
*a **wild** horse, a **wild** temper*

wilderness wild land where no one lives

wilful wanting to do something, even though other people say it is wrong
*a **wilful** child*

will 1 a kind of letter left by someone who has died. It tells people what he wants to be done with his money and things.
2 the power to choose what you want to do
3 is going to
*He **will** be nine tomorrow.*
*We**'ll** soon be there.*
*I said I **would** be late.*
*I**'d** like another sweater.*

willing ready and happy to do what is wanted

willow a kind of tree that grows near water and has thin branches that bend easily

wily crafty
a **wily** fox

win 1 to get a prize
2 to beat someone else in a game
We've **won** four games and lost two.

wince to move slightly because you are upset or in pain

wind[1] (*rhymes with* grinned) air moving along quickly

wind[2] (*rhymes with* blind)
1 to turn a key to make a machine work
The clock started when she **wound** it.
2 to wrap cloth, thread, tape, or string tightly around something

windmill a mill that uses wind to make its machinery work. It has blades fixed to it like a fan and the wind makes these turn.

window an opening in the wall of a building. It is filled with glass and lets in light.

wine a strong drink usually made from grapes

wing one of the parts of a bird or insect used for flying
a pair of **wings**

wink to close and open one eye quickly

winter the coldest part of the year

wipe to rub something with a cloth to dry it or clean it

wire a long, thin strip of metal that can be bent into different shapes

wisdom the ability to understand many things

wise able to understand many things

wish to say or think what you would like to happen

wisp a little bit of straw, hair, or smoke

witch a woman who uses magic to do bad things. Witches in fairy stories have tall, black, pointed hats and ride in the air on brooms.

with 1 having
*a man **with** a long coat*
2 in the company of
*I came **with** a friend.*
3 using
*It was written **with** a pen.*
4 against
*fighting **with** the enemy*

wither to dry up and get paler and smaller
***withered** flowers*

without not having
***without** any money*

witness someone who sees something important happen

witty clever and funny

wives more than one wife

wizard a man in fairy stories, who can do magic things

wobble to shake or rock. Jelly wobbles.

woke, woken see **wake**

wolf a wild animal like a big, fierce dog
*a pack of **wolves***

woman a fully grown female
*The three **women** were sisters.*

won see **win**

wonder 1 a feeling of surprise because of something strange or marvellous
2 to ask yourself about something
*I **wonder** who did it.*

wonderful so good that it surprises you
*a **wonderful** holiday*

won't *a short form for* will not

wood 1 the branches and trunks of trees cut up so that they can be used for making things or burned in fires
2 a lot of trees growing together

woodchuck see **groundhog**

wooden made of wood

wood pecker a bird that eats insects living in tree trunks. It has a strong beak for making holes in wood and a long, sticky tongue for catching insects.

woodwork making things out of wood
a **woodwork** *lesson*

wool the thick, soft hair that covers sheep. It is spun into thread and used for making cloth and for knitting.

woollen made of wool

word a sound or group of sounds that means something when you say it, write it, or read it

word processor a machine connected to a computer that types letters and other information automatically

wore see **wear**

work a job or something else that you have to do

worker a person paid to work with his hands, a tool, or a machine

workshop a place where things are made or mended

world the earth or anything else in space that is like it

worm a long, thin creature that wriggles about in the soil

worn see **wear**

worry to be upset because you are thinking about something bad that might happen

worse more seriously, bad
*The fire damage was **worse** at the back of the house.*

worship to love and praise

worst most seriously bad
*He's the **worst** in the class for talking too much.*

worth with a certain value
*This old stamp is **worth** $100.*

worthless not worth anything

would see **will**

wound¹ (woond)
an injury from something like a knife or a bullet

wound² (*rhymes with* sound)
see **wind**²

wove, woven see **weave**

wrap to put cloth or paper around something

wrath (rath)
anger

wreath flowers or leaves twisted together into a ring
a holly **wreath**

wreck 1 to damage a ship, building, or car so badly that it cannot be used again
2 a ship, building, or car so badly damaged that it cannot be used again

wren a very small, brown bird

wrench a tool for turning nuts and bolts

wrestle to struggle with someone

wretched (retch-id)
1 unhappy or ill
2 poor
wretched *health*

wriggle to twist and turn the body about like a worm

wring to squeeze and twist something wet to get the water out of it

He washed the towel and **wrung** *it.*

wrinkle a small crease in the skin. Old people usually have a lot of wrinkles.

wrist the thin part of the arm where it is joined to the hand

write to put words or signs on paper so that people can read them
I **wrote** *to her last week.*
You have **written** *this very neatly.*

writhe to twist or roll about because you are in great pain

writing something that has been written
untidy **writing**
a piece of **writing**

written see **write**

wrong not right
the **wrong** *answer*

wrote see **write**

wrung see **wring**

x-ray a special photograph that shows the inside of a body so that doctors can see if there is anything wrong

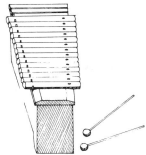

xylophone (zeye-la-fone)
a row of bars that you hit with
small hammers to make
musical sounds

Yy

yacht (yot)

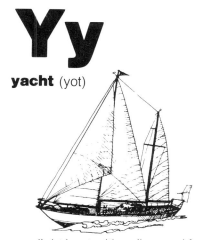

a light boat with sails, used for
racing

yard 1 ground that is next to a
building and has a wall or a
fence around it
2 a special area for certain
work
a railroad yard

yawn to open your mouth wide
because you are tired

year a measure for time. A year
is twelve months or three
hundred and sixty-five years.

yell to shout

yelp to give a quick, shrill cry like
a dog in pain

yesterday the day before today

yet 1 up to now
*The rain has not yet begun to
fall.*
2 by now
Aren't you finished yet?

yield 1 to give in
*The tree finally yielded to the
strong wind and fell over.*
2 the amount of fruit or grain on
a plant
a good yield of apples

yodel to shout with a musical
sound, changing from a low
note to a high note and back
again

yoghurt a thick liquid made
from sour milk. It usually has
fruit in it and you eat it with a
spoon.

yoke a long, curved piece of
wood put over the necks of two
oxen to help them pull the cart

231

yolk (*rhymes with* joke)
the round, yellow part of an egg

you the person or people you are speaking to
You are reading these words.

young born not long ago. A kitten is a young cat.

youngster someone who is young

your belonging to you
your book

yourself, yourselves 1 you and no one else
2 by yourself, by yourselves on your own

youth 1 a boy or young man
2 the time in your life when you are young

yo-yo a toy made of a flat spool with string wound around in the centre of it. You can make the spool move up and down the string.

zero the number nothing, also written 0

zig-zag a line with sudden turns in it like this

zinc a bluish-white metal that does not rust easily

zinnia a large colourful flower with many petals

zipper a special fastener for joining two edges of material together. Some dresses, trousers, and bags have zippers.

zone a part of a town, country, or the world that is special in some way
a parking zone

zoo a place where different kinds of wild animals are kept so that people can go and see them

zoom to move very quickly

Zz

zebra an animal like a horse with black and white stripes. Zebras are found in Africa.

NUMBERS

1	one	first
2	two	second
3	three	third
4	four	fourth
5	five	fifth
6	six	sixth
7	seven	seventh
8	eight	eighth
9	nine	ninth
10	ten	tenth
11	eleven	eleventh
12	twelve	twelfth
13	thirteen	thirteenth
14	fourteen	fourteenth
15	fifteen	fifteenth
16	sixteen	sixteenth
17	seventeen	seventeenth
18	eighteen	eighteenth
19	nineteen	nineteenth
20	twenty	twentieth
21	twenty-one	twenty-first
22	twenty-two	twenty-second
30	thirty	thirtieth
40	forty	fortieth
50	fifty	fiftieth
60	sixty	sixtieth
70	seventy	seventieth
80	eighty	eightieth
90	ninety	ninetieth
100	a hundred	hundredth
101	a hundred and one	hundred and first
200	two hundred	two hundredth
1,000	a thousand	thousandth
1,000,000	a million	millionth

FLAT SHAPES

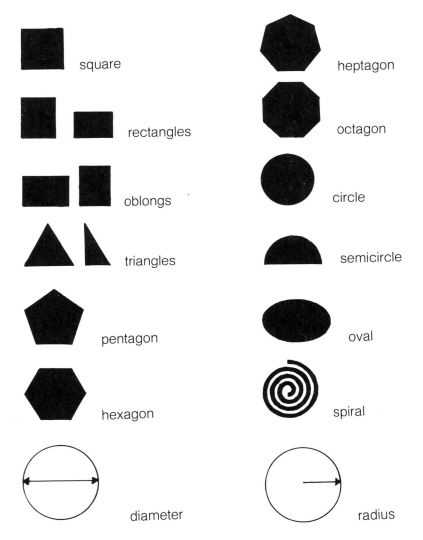

square

rectangles

oblongs

triangles

pentagon

hexagon

diameter

heptagon

octagon

circle

semicircle

oval

spiral

radius

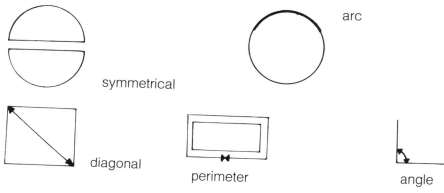

symmetrical

arc

diagonal

perimeter

angle

SOLID SHAPES

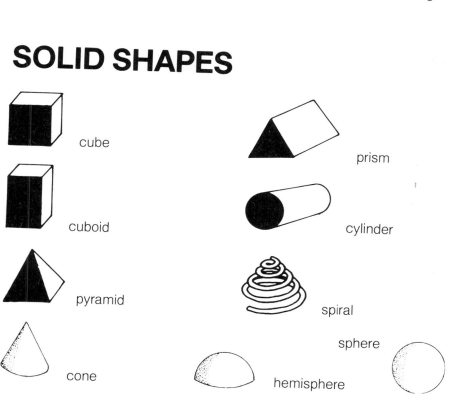

cube

prism

cuboid

cylinder

pyramid

spiral

cone

sphere

hemisphere

CONTINENTS

Africa
Antarctica
Asia
Australia

Europe
North America
South America

OCEANS

Antarctic
Arctic
Atlantic

Indian
Pacific

PLANETS

Mercury
Venus
Earth
Mars
Jupiter

Saturn
Uranus
Neptune
Pluto

DAYS

Sunday
Monday
Tuesday
Wednesday

Thursday
Friday
Saturday

MONTHS

January (31 days)
February (28 days)*
March (31 days)
April (30 days)
May (31 days)
June (30 days)

July (31 days)
August (31 days)
September (30 days)
October (31 days)
November (30 days)
December (31 days)

*Every four years, February has 29 days.
These years are called LEAP YEARS.

PROVINCES AND TERRITORIES OF CANADA	CAPITAL CITIES	BECAME A PROVINCE
ALBERTA	EDMONTON	1905
BRITISH COLUMBIA	VICTORIA	1871
MANITOBA	WINNIPEG	1870
NEW BRUNSWICK	FREDERICTON	1867
NEWFOUNDLAND	ST. JOHN'S	1949
NOVA SCOTIA	HALIFAX	1867
ONTARIO	TORONTO	1867
PRINCE EDWARD ISLAND	CHARLOTTETOWN	1873
QUEBEC	QUEBEC CITY	1867
SASKATCHEWAN	REGINA	1905
YUKON	WHITEHORSE	—
NORTHWEST TERRITORIES	YELLOWKNIFE	—

PRIME MINISTERS OF CANADA

NAME	IN OFFICE	PARTY
SIR JOHN A. MACDONALD	JULY 1, 1867 NOV. 5, 1873	CONSERVATIVE
ALEXANDER MACKENZIE	NOV. 7, 1873 OCT. 9, 1878	LIBERAL
SIR JOHN A. MACDONALD	OCT. 17, 1878 JUNE 6, 1891	CONSERVATIVE
SIR JOHN J.C. ABBOTT	JUNE 16, 1891 NOV. 24, 1892	CONSERVATIVE
SIR JOHN S.D. THOMPSON	DEC. 5, 1892 DEC. 12, 1894	CONSERVATIVE
SIR MACKENZIE BOWELL	DEC. 21, 1894 APR. 27, 1896	CONSERVATIVE
SIR CHARLES TUPPER	MAY 1, 1896 JULY 8, 1896	CONSERVATIVE
SIR WILFRID LAURIER	JULY 11, 1896 OCT. 6, 1911	LIBERAL
SIR ROBERT BORDEN	OCT. 10, 1911 OCT. 12, 1917	CONSERVATIVE
	OCT. 12, 1917 JULY 10, 1920	UNION GOVERNMENT
ARTHUR MEIGHEN	JULY 10, 1920 DEC. 29, 1921	CONSERVATIVE

W.L. MACKENZIE KING	DEC. 29, 1921 JUNE 28, 1926	LIBERAL
ARTHUR MEIGHEN	JUNE 29, 1926 SEPT. 25, 1926	CONSERVATIVE
W.L. MACKENZIE KING	SEPT. 25, 1926 AUG. 6, 1930	LIBERAL
R.B. BENNETT	AUG. 7, 1930 OCT. 23, 1935	CONSERVATIVE
W.L. MACKENZIE KING	OCT. 23, 1935 NOV. 15, 1948	LIBERAL
LOUIS S. ST. LAURENT	NOV. 15, 1948 JUNE 21, 1957	LIBERAL
JOHN G. DIEFENBAKER	JUNE 21, 1957 APRIL 22, 1963	CONSERVATIVE
LESTER B. PEARSON	APRIL 22, 1963 APRIL 20, 1968	LIBERAL
PIERRE E. TRUDEAU	APRIL 20, 1968 JUNE 4, 1979	LIBERAL
JOE CLARK	JUNE 4, 1979 MARCH 3, 1980	CONSERVATIVE
PIERRE E. TRUDEAU	MARCH 3, 1980	LIBERAL